THE WEST COAST
BED &
BREAKFAST
GUIDE

Villa St. Helena, in the California Wine Country.

CALIFORNIA, OREGON, AND WASHINGTON

Bed & Breakfast Guide

WEST COAST

BY COURTIA WORTH AND TERRY BERGER

Photographs by Will Faller

DESIGNED AND PRODUCED BY ROBERT R. REID
AND TERRY BERGER

PRENTICE HALL PRESS
NEW YORK

FRONTISPIECE PHOTOGRAPH:
Dining room at Morey Mansion, Redlands, California.

Editorial assistance by Michele Sensale.
Map by Anthony St. Aubyn.

Published by Prentice Hall Press
A Division of Simon & Schuster, Inc.
Gulf + Western Building
One Gulf + Western Plaza
New York, New York 10023

━━━━━━━━━━━━━━━━━━━━━━━━━━━━━━━

A Robert Reid/Terry Berger production
Typeset in Bodoni Book by Monotype Composition Company, Baltimore.
Printed and bound by Mandarin Offset Marketing (H.K.) Ltd, Hong Kong.

1 2 3 4 5 6 7 8 9 10

Library of Congress Cataloging-in-Publication Data

Worth, Courtia.
     The West Coast bed & breakfast guide.

     1. Bed and breakfast accommodations—California—Di-
rectories. 2. Bed and breakfast accommodations—Oregon—
Directories. 3. Bed and breakfast accommodations—Wash-
ington (State)—Directories. I. Berger, Terry. II. Title. III.
Title: West Coast bed and breakfast guide.
TX907.W694 1986   647′.9479   86-17025

ISBN 0-671-62946-8

CONTENTS

Northern California

Oregon

Washington

AUTHORS' NOTE

Staying at Bed & Breakfasts is an adventurous form of travel. It affords an opportunity to meet people who are happy to share their extraordinary home or inn and their intimate knowledge of the area.

Unlike the European tradition of a single room in a private home, most bed and breakfast establishments in this country are usually housed in a historical or architecturally interesting building, with from two to ten guest rooms. Decorated with antiques, handcrafted furnishings, or collectibles from one era or another, they provide an intimate setting for business travel, a special occasion, or a romantic weekend. They are professional in maintaining high standards of hospitality, housekeeping, food preparation, and business etiquette.

A key to the front door is usually provided and guests have free access to the living and dining areas as well as patios, lawns, and porches. Keys to individual guest rooms are unusual. There is often sherry, wine, tea or coffee available, and sometimes fruit or sweets in the rooms.

Breakfasts, which are included in room rates, provide guests with an opportunity to meet other travelers, trade stories, or share in adventures. The food ranges from simple continental fare such as juice, coffee, tea, and croissants to elaborate two and three course meals that include quiches, omelets, hot meats, and savories. The food is generally fresh, tasty, and elegantly presented as hosts welcome this opportunity to entertain their guests.

Check in times are to be respected and a call to your host if your arrival will be delayed is advisable. As cancellations create havoc for the small establishment, individual policies should be noted and adhered to. Shared bathrooms are often found in historic homes, and when everyone is considerate, rarely is anyone inconvenienced. Guests are expected to treat the host's home as their own or that of a friend's.

Normally children are not part of the Bed & Breakfast world, although many innkeepers do welcome older well-behaved children. Pets are rarely, if ever, allowed. Smoking is a real issue and smokers should note that the majority of inns do not allow smoking in bedrooms and a great many do not allow smoking inside the inn.

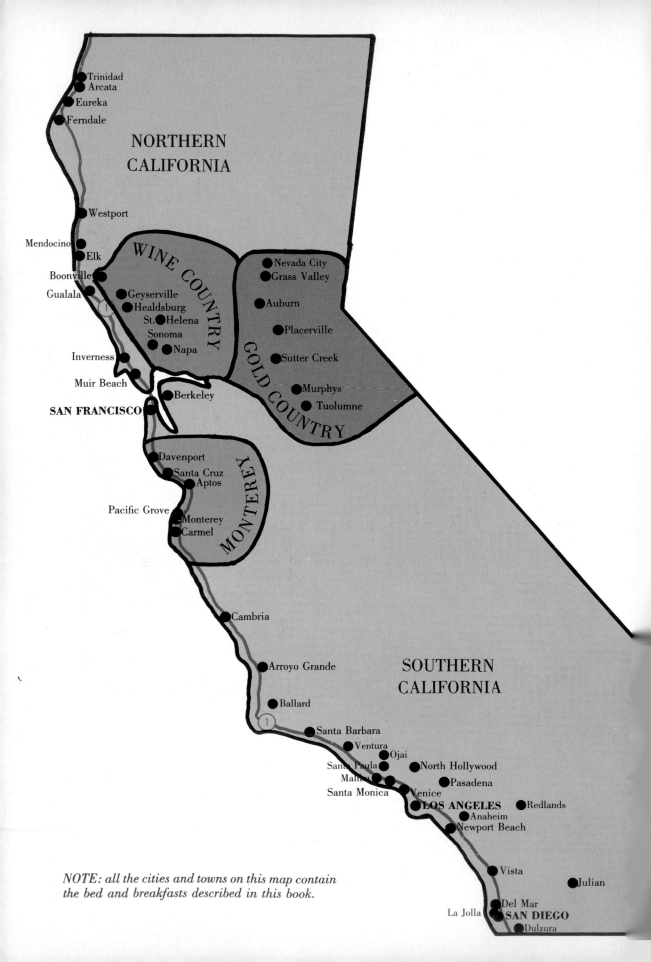

NORTHERN
CALIFORNIA

Trinidad
Arcata
Eureka
Ferndale

Westport

Mendocino
Elk
Boonville
Gualala

WINE COUNTRY

Geyserville
Healdsburg
St. Helena
Sonoma
Napa

Nevada City
Grass Valley

Auburn

Placerville

Sutter Creek

Murphys
Tuolumne

GOLD COUNTRY

Inverness

Muir Beach

Berkeley

SAN FRANCISCO

Davenport
Santa Cruz
Aptos

Pacific Grove

Monterey
Carmel

MONTEREY

Cambria

Arroyo Grande

Ballard

SOUTHERN
CALIFORNIA

Santa Barbara
Ventura
Ojai
Santa Paula
Malibu
Santa Monica

North Hollywood
Pasadena

Venice
LOS ANGELES
Anaheim
Newport Beach

Redlands

Vista

Julian

Del Mar
La Jolla SAN DIEGO
Dulzura

*NOTE: all the cities and towns on this map contain
the bed and breakfasts described in this book.*

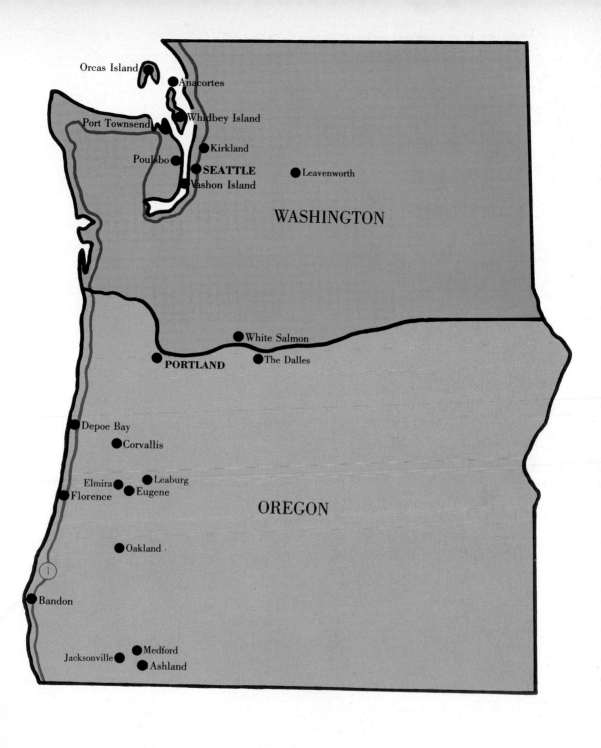

Orcas Island

Anacortes

Port Townsend

Whidbey Island

Kirkland

Poulsbo

SEATTLE

Vashon Island

Leavenworth

WASHINGTON

White Salmon

PORTLAND

The Dalles

Depoe Bay

Corvallis

Elmira

Leaburg

Florence

Eugene

OREGON

Oakland

Bandon

Jacksonville

Medford

Ashland

SOUTHERN CALIFORNIA

THE COTTAGE

Cottage hideaway in San Diego

Fresh fruit and nuts await guests.

A stroll down a walkway beside the main house leads to a secluded hideaway with several fruit trees framing the doorway. Lovingly decorated with turn-of-the-century furnishings, the house boasts an oak pump organ that works, a three-foot-high coffee grinder that promises to produce a fine blend, and a potbellied wood-burning stove that takes the chill out of the morning air.

A tap on your door in the morning and breakfast appears: a tray of steaming hot bread, fresh fruit, and coffee or tea, along with a morning paper. It is easy to grow fond of this intimate, self-contained house, with bedroom, sitting room, kitchen, small dining area, and private bath. Within walking distance of shops and restaurants, five minutes by car from the San Diego Zoo and Balboa Park, and thirty minutes from Mexico, you are well located to make the most of your stay.

THE COTTAGE, P.O. Box 3292, San Diego, CA 92103; (619) 299-1564; Carol and Robert Emerick, hosts. One cottage with a king-size bed in bedroom and a single bed in living room. Rates: single $45, double $50, triple $60. Includes generous continental breakfast. No pets; Visa/MasterCard; no smoking permitted.

DIRECTIONS: contact hosts.

Antiques, including a working pump organ, furnish the Cottage.

One of seven 19th century houses restored and moved to San Diego's Heritage Park.

HERITAGE PARK

In the heart of Old Town

Heritage Park Bed and Breakfast is one of the endangered Victorian houses that was literally cut in half and rejoined, along with seven others, at Heritage Park Victorian Village. The house is an 1889 Queen Anne, characterized by a two-story corner tower and encircling veranda. The Village is part of San Diego's historic Old Town, and is adjacent to the famous Presidio Park Plaza, Museum, Adobe Chapel, and other buildings.

Unusual touches throughout the house include a collection of antique dresses, an intricate Victorian wedding gown in The Queen Anne Room, and a double Lover's Knot Canopy over a four-poster double bed in the Country Heart Room.

What guests love most about this B & B is a special dinner service for "en suite" dining. The choice is between a Victorian country supper or a five course candlelight dinner. The country supper consisting of barbequed ribs or chicken, salads, baked apples, and cheese croissants is delivered all at once, thus allowing total privacy while dining. The candlelight dinner, on the other hand, comes complete with butler and chambermaid in authentic period clothing. Over the course of two hours they graciously serve a gourmet feast beginning with filo pastries and ending with cream liqueur.

In the evenings after wine and cheese, guests gather in the rose-colored parlor to view vintage films such as "It's a Wonderful Life" or "His Girl Friday". For the B & B guests here it is a wonderful life!

HERITAGE PARK, 2470 Heritage Park Row, San Diego, CA 92110; (619) 295-7088; Lori Chandler, proprietress; Aviva Hostetter, host. Nine rooms, three with private bath. Rates: $65 to $105. Includes elaborate breakfast delivered to your door or served on the front veranda. Turn down service and long stem chocolate roses on each pillow. French spoken; no pets; no children under 14; smoking on the veranda; handicap access and accommodations; MasterCard/Visa.

DIRECTIONS: from downtown and airport: I-5 north to Old Town Avenue offramp. Left on Old Town Avenue, right on Harney to Heritage Park. From LA: I-5 to Old Town Avenue offramp. Left on San Diego Avenue and right on Harney.

A classic wood stove warms the lobby, where breakfast is served.

JULIAN HOTEL

Well-worn character

In the 1870s the first discoveries of gold were made a few hundred yards from the Julian Hotel, which stands today as the sole surviving hostelry to have lived through the glory of the mining boom. Each of the many rooms off the long hallways retains the full flavor of the frontier, and one senses there haven't been a great many changes since the original guests polished their pistols here. Well-worn character prevails over fancy frills, and the visitor should not object to the shared "necessary rooms for ladies and gentlemen" down the hall.

Breakfast is served on card tables set up in the lobby across from the wood-burning stove. And one can browse through the original guest registers dating back a hundred years to the time when the hotel was built by freed slaves.

While in this classic, false-front western town, you might enjoy the Wildflower Festival in the spring, or the Banjo and Fiddle Festival in the fall. Whatever the time of year, the apple pie is a treat to be considered seriously at any of the local restaurants.

JULIAN HOTEL, P.O. Box 856, Julian, CA 92036; (619) 765-0201; Steve and Gig Ballinger, owners; Jean and Mary Thompson, managers. Sixteen rooms, shared and private baths, and a Honeymoon Cottage. Open all year. Rates: weeknights $26 to $58; weekends $30 to $85. Includes full breakfast. Children under sixteen during week; no pets; no credit cards; smoking permitted.

DIRECTIONS: from L.A. take I-5 south to Rte. 78 east through Escondido to Julian (3½ hrs.). From San Diego, take I-8 east to Rte. 79 north to Julian (1½ hrs.).

BROOKSIDE FARM

Thirty miles from Mexico

Brookside Farm offers the quaint pleasure of fetching brown eggs for breakfast from the Guishard's cooperative chickens and a dramatic three-level terrace that is the gathering place for guests from morning coffee to late afternoon, under the shade of an ancient and gigantic California live oak.

Closest to the brook, on the third tier of the terrace are two guest rooms, The Washroom and The Kitchen, which are more rustic than the romantic Rose Room on the second floor, with its thick pink carpet, lace tablecloths, rose colored wallpaper, and panoramic view of the mountains. The Attic Room, with its oak rocker and original linoleum floor, has the finest view of the brook, and the brightest room, The Sun Room, is just off the dining room.

The living room is fronted with a bank of windows accented with royal blue stained glass made by Edd. The earth colored Tecate Brick floor (made in Mexico just thirty miles to the south) and wood stove all add to the homey feel of this rural retreat.

BROOKSIDE FARM, 1373 Marron Valley Road, Dulzura, CA 92017; (619) 468-3043; Edd and Judy Guishard, hosts. Nine rooms, two with private baths. Rates: $45 to $65. Includes full varied breakfast such as California omelets with Ortega peppers and homemade biscuits, or blueberry pancakes with homemade sausage (exceptional!) Country Fare buffet often served on Sundays. Gourmet homestyle dinner by reservation. Country Weekend, $135, includes breakfast, dinners, and picnic lunch. No children; no pets; guests may smoke in the living room; no credit cards.

DIRECTIONS: from San Diego: follow Rte. 94 to Dulzura; 1½ miles past Dulzura Café, turn right on Marron Valley Road. 40 minutes south of San Diego.

The Sun Room.

The bungalow overlooks town and tides.

ROCK HAUS

Spectacular sunsets

As soon as you step onto the enclosed veranda and take in its panoramic view of the ocean, you'll know you have stopped at a special place. Rock Haus is inviting for breakfast and awesome at sunset, and the day can be spent walking on the beach, browsing through the fancy shops, or cheering on your favorite Thoroughbred at the Del Mar Racetrack.

This landmark 1910 bungalow-style house has a large and welcoming living room, where wine is served from the host's personal wine cellar. Rooms named Whale Watch, Wicker Garden, and Court Room, among others, have been meticulously decorated, each with individual charm and character.

ROCK HAUS, 410 15th Street, Del Mar, CA 92014; (619) 481-3764; Carol & Tom Hauser, hosts. Ten rooms, four with private baths and two with private entry on ground floor. Rates: $75 to $125, slightly less during the week. Includes continental breakfast and wine in the evening. Visa/MasterCard/Discover; no children, pets, or smoking. Situated in the heart of Del Mar village; shops & beach are just a short walk away.

DIRECTIONS: from I-5 exit at Via de la Valle and head west to Jimmy Durante Blvd. Take a left and feed into US-101. Take a left on 15th Street.

Peace and tranquility.

LA JOLLA

Steps away from seaside and shopping

With its air of sophistication and gentility, this fine bed and breakfast is perfectly suited to La Jolla. Artfully designed arches provide an entry to the house and gardens. The mood is so serene it is difficult to imagine that it is located on the periphery of the bustle of La Jolla's fancy shops and gourmet restaurants.

Special attention has gone into decorating the rooms. Each has a distinctive personality and flavor. Holiday, the master suite at the front of the house, is bright and spacious. Tall windows, a fireplace, a four poster canopy bed, white couch and wing chairs add elegance and warmth. The Cove, with a more casual feeling, has warm peach walls, white wicker furniture, and a salmon and blue Dhurrie rug. Branches of trees can be seen blooming outside in the courtyard. Altogether different, and slightly masculine in tone, the Garden Room opens onto the courtyard. Although the walls are pale lavender, the hunter green plaid wool comforter, handsomely painted rural folk art over the mantel, and rustic fireplace combine to make this room more like a den.

The Irving Gill Penthouse features a separate living room and an open sun deck, which in addition to the window seat and couch in the bedroom, lends itself to entertaining.

For the pleasure of all the guests, there is a sitting room on the second floor of the original house which is vibrant during the day with its cool white walls and lavender accents. Tall arched windows welcome Southern California sun and a deck off the sitting room draws sunworshippers. The sitting room serves guests well in the evening too, whether it is to watch a bit of news on television or step out on the deck to gaze at the stars.

THE BED & BREAKFAST INN AT LA JOLLA, 7753 Draper Avenue, La Jolla, CA 92037; (619) 456-2066; Betty Albee, Sixteen charming rooms, all with private baths, several with sea view and fireplaces. Rates: $65 to $150. Includes a light continental breakfast delivered to your room or served in the dining room. Tennis courts 100 feet away. La Jolla Museum of Art across the street and shops and ocean less than a minute's walk. No children under 12; no pets; Visa/MasterCard.

DIRECTIONS: from the north or south: from I-5 take La Jolla Village Drive west. Left onto Torrey Pines Road for 3 miles and turn right onto Prospect Place. Go 10 blocks and bear left onto Draper Avenue across from Museum. It is the 2nd house on the left.

Overleaf, the original splendor of the house, with all its elaborate details.

MOREY MANSION

A magnificent accomplishment

Master shipbuilder and craftsman David Morey built this mansion as testimony of love to his wife Sarah. The exterior of the house, built in 1889, is extraordinary in its combination of styles. The Russian Orthodox onion dome, French mansard roof of the two story tower, the English fan over the front stairway, the Italian balustrades, and the Chinese-style veranda, all painted in various tones of browns and beiges accented with green, combine to make Morey Mansion breathtaking. Even the windows change from one story to the next, from traditional to arched to gothic. In the daylight the structure is massive; at dusk it glows with subtle lighting; at night it glistens like a fairy-tale castle.

Fortunately, the elegance of the home remains unspoiled inside and out. Leaded beveled glass windows imported from Belgium in the front bay windows of the parlor and dining room are beautifully preserved. The original burgundy velvet Parisian portiers trimmed with tapestry still hang in the parlor. All the parlor furniture is carved with Grecian women to match Morley's carvings on the fireplace. In the circular bay there is a grand player piano, with each key able to sound twenty volumes, and a working original Edison record player.

Much of the house tells the story of Morey's wife Sarah, who sold thousands of orange seedlings to raise the twenty thousand dollars that made this dream house possible. Carvings of orange blossoms are everywhere, in the wood and on every piece of hardware in the house, from the doorknobs to the drawer pulls.

To stay in this mansion is to experience first hand the life of one who was prosperous, imaginative, highly skilled, and deeply in love.

MOREY MANSION, 190 Terracina Boulevard, Redlands, CA 92373; (714) 793-7970 for recorded message with information and brochure request; 714-793-7870 for reservations; Carl Ljunguist & Gary Conway, proprietors. Seven rooms: four master bedrooms, sharing two baths; two smaller rooms with private baths; separate guest house. Rates: $70 to $95. Includes a full breakfast in formal dining room, and high tea in the parlor. Smoking permitted on the porches. No children under 14; no pets; reservations confirmed with Visa/MasterCard/American Express, but payment with personal checks is preferred.

DIRECTIONS: midway between Los Angeles and Palm Springs on I-10, six miles east of San Bernardino, Take Alabama exit south, follow "H" (hospital) signs. 2.6 miles to Terracina and Olive Ave.

DORYMAN'S INN

Total luxury
at Newport Beach

It is immediately apparent that no expense or comfort was spared in the execution of this extraordinary bed and breakfast. As you step off the street into a small vestibule, a receding oak door exposes an expansive gold leaf mirror, luminous brass railing, quartersawed wainscoting, silk wallpaper, and rich wool carpeting. You have just stepped into the elevator at Doryman's Inn.

Upon arriving at the second floor, you are ushered along a skylighted hallway to one of the opulent rooms. Appointments include Italian mar-

ble fireplaces, luxurious window seats, antique furnishings, and artwork collected from all over the world.

The effort to please is apparent, whether you take the celebrity suite facing the ocean, with the sitting area, four-poster, conference table, and marble Jacuzzi, or the room with the ocean view and the rosette pleated canopy. One-way glass has been installed in all of the windows to ensure total privacy, walls are insulated, and doors are two-and-a-half-inches of solid oak. Bedside controls raise or lower gas-fueled fireplaces that glow in all the rooms, and each of the marble bathrooms has a fern-filled skylight, sunken tub, and telephone.

A buffet-style full breakfast is served in the parlor and may be eaten there or elsewhere. Other features of this 1921 landmark building include a redwood sun deck and Jacuzzi for eight on top of the complex, and Rex's fine restaurant on the ground floor. As if that weren't enough, Doryman's is located right at the beach and boardwalk of Newport Pier.

DORYMAN'S INN, 2102 W. Ocean Front, Newport Beach, CA 92663; (714) 675-7300; Mr. and Mrs. Richard Lawrence, owners; Bill Nisson, Julian Rigotti, Michael Politz, hosts. French and Italian spoken. Ten rooms with private baths, including two Jacuzzis. Rates: $120 to $225. Includes an expanded continental breakfast. No children under 14; no pets; all major cards.
DIRECTIONS: located at the base of Newport Pier.

Friendly service at the front desk.

TERRACE MANOR

A Tudor mansion of magic and mystery

This English Tudor mansion was built in 1902 for a prominent glass and hardwood manufacturer, and every bit of it reflects his uncompromising use of the finest and most glorious materials available. Starting with the front door, with its oval beveled and leaded glass, the use of glass throughout the house becomes increasingly breathtaking. A 3 × 6 foot wall of turquoise colored glass in a fleur de lis pattern shimmers with luminosity over the staircase. A window bedazzles in gold with crimson flowers and emerald foliage.

The dark, deep burgundy walls and thick hunter green carpet throughout the house combine with bold, Rousseau-like floral pink and green wallpaper in the dining room to recapture the color scheme predominant in the Victorian era. The paneled oak stairway, the Philippine mahogany wainscoting, and the Ionic columned dining room fireplace all exhibit the builder's discriminating good taste and fortuitous resources.

Host Sandy is known to perform magic at the breakfast table. He and Shirley are members of the famed Magic Castle, and offer guests complimentary passes to an evening of entertainment at the private club of the Academy of Magical Arts.

TERRACE MANOR, 1353 Alvarado Terrace, Los Angeles, CA 90006; (213) 381-1478; Sandy & Shirley Spillman, hosts. Five rooms, each with private bath. One suite with trundle bed on sunporch. Rates: $55 to $85. Includes elaborate breakfast, such as Scotch eggs or bread made with figs from the tree in the yard. No children or pets. Smoking on porch or patio. Located in downtown area several blocks from the Convention Center. Off-street parking.

DIRECTIONS: from LAX Airport take Century Blvd. east for 8 miles to Harbor Freeway (US-110). Go north on Harbor to Santa Monica Freeway West (US 10). Get into left hand lane for Pico offramp which comes up immediately as you enter the Santa Monica Freeway. On Pico, turn left (west) to Alvarado Terrace.

Exquisite stained glass casts a warm glow into the entry hall.

The owner's 1940 LaSalle is perfectly appropriate. Overleaf, Laguna Beach.

EASTLAKE INN

Always something to celebrate

Eastlake Inn sits on a hillside in Angelino Heights, known for its extraordinary community of Victorian houses built between 1886 to 1888.

Located in downtown Los Angeles, this "celebration inn" appeals to tourists who want to be near museums, business people who need quick freeway access, and adventurous travelers seeking a unique experience. Hosts Murray and Planaria invite guests to explore ways of having fun which far surpass the average birthday or anniversary celebration. The Eastlake catalog of possibilities features a limousine driven tour of L.A.'s best ice cream and chocolate spots, a hot air balloon flight, a chamber music concert in your room, a trail ride to a Mexican restaurant for dinner and margaritas, and an airplane tour of the Grand Canyon. Holidays provide extra opportunities for fun: the Soaring Heights Valentine Celebration features a twilight gondola ride to the music of Verdi and Puccini; Christmas brings a homespun rendering of Dickens' "A Christmas Carol," complete with plum pudding and Jacob Marley clanking down the stairs, and Halloween . . . well, some things should remain surprises.

The master suite has a spacious sitting room, carved mahogany furniture covered in deep green velvet and a large writing desk, as well as a sunroom with white lace covered day-bed overlooking a fragrant lemon tree. Planaria's Dream, a bedroom on the main floor, is decorated in soothing white and biege tones with a brilliant scarlet red fainting couch situated under the bay window.

To avoid marring the old pine floorboards, ladies are asked to leave their high heels at the door. All are reminded, however, to keep their enthusiasm with them—at all times!

EASTLAKE INN, 1442 Kellam Avenue, Los Angeles, CA 90026; (213) 250-1620; Murray Burns & Planaria Price, hosts. Five rooms, four share three baths, one with private bath. Rates: $45 to $90. Includes breakfast served in the dining room, in your room, or best of all, in bed. Smoking permitted on the porches. Children over 11. Off-street parking. Languages: French, Italian, Canadian, Irish, and Australian!

DIRECTIONS: from the Hollywood Freeway (US-101) exit at Glendale. From the east, take a left onto Temple Street and then a left onto East Edgeware Rd. Proceed to Carroll and take a left. Right on Douglas and left on Kellam. From the west; exit at Glendale and make a right onto Bellevue. Proceed to East Edgeware and make a left. Then left on Carrol, right on Douglas and left on Kellam.

ANAHEIM COUNTRY INN

Welcome to Disneyland

Rainbows dance across the dining room table and onto the rose carpeted living room floor as the sun pours through this inn's bevelled leaded glass windows. The architecturally grand home with over five thousand square feet of space was built in 1910 for John Cool, a German farmer who primarily raised grapes. As a lark he planted ten avocado trees, and his success was the beginning of a whole new industry. He loved to cook for his friends, especially the bounty from his hunting and fishing expeditions, so the Princess Anne home became famous in Anaheim as the scene of many gala parties.

Whether it's lounging on a porch swing or trying a round of horseshoes, the grounds never cease to be festive and inviting. A favorite spot to relax in is the spa under the massive Mulberry tree or in a big chair on the rounded front porch. Thirty different kinds of roses blossom in the garden and herbs, camelias, and azaleas are bountiful.

Three blocks from the house is a stop for a "FunBus" which wisks visitors off to Disneyland, Knotts Berry Farm with its own western style rides, ghost town and gold panning activity, and to the Convention Center.

ANAHEIM COUNTRY INN, 856 South Walnut, Anaheim, CA 92802; (714) 778-0150; Lois Ramont and Marilyn Watson, hosts. Nine rooms, one with private bath. Rates: $32 to $100. Includes a hearty breakfast and an afternoon social hour. Outdoor spa. Children over 12; no pets; smoking on outside porches. Off-street parking; laundry facilities for guests. One mile from Disneyland.

DIRECTIONS: from the north from I-5, take Ball Road exit west to the 2nd light and make a right onto Walnut. Proceed 3 blocks to the house on the corner.

CASA ALMA

A whitewashed oasis of folk art

High, whitewashed walls surrounding homes always pique one's curiosity. Upon entering the courtyard of this Mediterranean villa, you can be assured of making intriguing discoveries.

For years the owners of Casa Alma have collected folk art and crafts from Central and South America. Adorning the living room are large, vibrantly colored yarn paintings by the Huichol Indians, and elaborate weavings hang throughout the house. Tin figurines, symbolic dolls, and pottery are casually displayed, and if you are at all interested in anthropology, the origin and meaning of each piece will be happily explained.

Hardly a modest affair, Casa Alma has two dining rooms, a television room, a large living room, and an entirely separate guest wing. At the same time guests are afforded the opportunity for privacy, they are offered all the warmth, comfort, and amenities of a private home.

Outdoors, a pool nestled amid flowers and blooming cactus is the center of an enchanting garden. The setting is so idyllic, in fact, that one is startled to be reminded that this home is located across from Will Rogers State Beach, one of California's most popular beaches, and a short way from Los Angeles.

CASA ALMA, Santa Monica, CA. Spanish spoken. Three rooms, one with private bath and two sharing. Spanish décor with sitting area and writing desk in each room. Rates: $65 double. Includes American or continental breakfast. Dog Lucky and two cats in residence. Smoking permitted. *Represented by Bed & Breakfast International.*

Hosts Alma and Joe at the hacienda entrance. Right, the grand entrance hall to Casa Alma.

LA MAIDA HOUSE

North Hollywood Mediterranean villa

Italian artisans, brought here in the 1920s, adorned this seven-thousand-square-foot Sicilian mansion with ironwork, woodwork, marble, and fountains. Built on a grand scale, it is a villa not unlike those found on the Mediterranean.

The splendor of magnolia trees, blooming orchids, and three hundred varieties of roses can be viewed from the stained-glass-covered solarium, while the grace of a former era is reflected in the expansive living room and a dining room that seats thirty-four. There are several casual niches for relaxing, among them a multitiered couch in the game room and an upstairs porch for intimate dining.

The rooms, filled with fresh flowers from La Maida's gardens, are airy and elegant. An especially glorious one, in the main house, is the Cipresso Suite, with a white-canopied four-poster bed, wicker chaise, mirrored dressing room, and large blue-tiled bathroom. Downstairs the sun pours through white lace curtains, creating beautiful shadows at arched windows. Adding to the warmth are the stained-glass windows designed and made by Megan Timothy, La Maida's hostess.

The windows only hint at Megan's artistry, for in addition to working with clay, stone, and fabric, she is a highly skilled cook. A beautifully presented continental breakfast is an introduction to epicurean dinners that Megan can arrange and prepare for you and your guests.

LA MAIDA HOUSE & BUNGALOWS, 11159 La Maida Street, North Hollywood, CA 91601; (818) 769-3857; Megan Timothy, hostess. Four rooms in main house; six in bungalos, all with private entrances, and several with Jacuzzi tubs and private gardens. Rates: $70 to $105. Includes generous continental breakfast. Phone and TV provided on request. Business and social affairs arranged. No children under sixteen; no pets; no smoking; no credit cards. A flock of elegant chickens provides fresh eggs.

DIRECTIONS: from Ventura Freeway 101, exit at Tujunga Blvd. Make a right and proceed to first light. Take a right on Camarillo Street, and proceed three blocks. Turn left onto Bellflower. Go one block to La Maida; the house is on the corner.

Left, the king-sized redwood, tile, and stained-glass bathroom of the Cipresso Suite. Above, extra-long beds in the Fontana Room.

A beautifully restored Craftsman bungalow.

SALISBURY HOUSE

Country charm in Los Angeles

A meticulous arrangement of porcelain dolls, family photographs, Victorian ornaments, baskets of flowers, and sparkling crystal surround you when you enter this 1910 craftsman-style house. Owners Kathleen Salisbury and her husband Bill have created this dream-come-true, magical oasis of warmth and laughter—quite unexpectedly in the heart of Los Angeles. Each guest room has its own personality, with turn-of-the-century memorabilia, stuffed animals, and assortments of sachets, potpourris, talcums, fragrant sprays, candles, and candies, carefully chosen to complement the color-coordinated décor. The top floor, with its pitched roof and freestanding tub, has its own special charm.

Piping hot Amaretto coffee appears in the morning in a silver urn on the mahogany sideboard. Elegant as the house may appear, you are welcome to wear your robe down to enjoy the Salisbury's full, hearty breakfast.

SALISBURY HOUSE, 2273 West 20th Street, Los Angeles, CA 90018; (213) 737-7817; Kathleen Salisbury, hostess. Five rooms, three with private bath. Rates: $55 to $70. Includes full breakfast and complimentary wine. No children under twelve; no pets; smoking permitted. Located downtown, near El Cholo, L.A.'s oldest Mexican restaurant.

DIRECTIONS: from Santa Monica Freeway (exit 10), go north on Western Avenue, turn left on 20th St.

The Attic Suite offers all the amenities.

The soft light of the seashore glows in Cora's Corner guest room.

VENICE BEACH HOUSE

Romantic lodgings near the beach

This recently restored house by the sea is a survivor of the splendid era of expansive two-story shingled beach houses, shaded verandas, and a more carefree way of life. Whether it is the breeze off the ocean, just steps away, or the genuine southern hospitality of the hostesses, mother and daughter, one feels privileged to have discovered the Venice Beach House.

Sophisticated décor enhances the romantic quality of this 1911 house, with its extensive use of wool wall coverings. The mood shifts from the contemporary elegance of the Pier Suite, a cool gray accented with rose, to Cora's Corner, a hot pink and white wicker room with a four-poster bed. The room named after town father Abbott Kinney is covered in Scottish plaid wool, hunter green carpet, and dark wainscoting.

An additional pleasure is bathing side by side in a large, lush bathroom in claw-foot tubs, or enjoying the double Jacuzzi adjacent to one of the suites. Breakfast on the veranda or in the sunny bay-window parlor usually includes a baked treat. You'll feel quite comfortable here, whether celebrating a special occasion or just looking for a lovely place in which to relax near the sea.

VENICE BEACH HOUSE, No. 15,Thirtieth Avenue, Venice, CA 90291; (213) 823-1966. Vivian and Phil Boesch, owners; Penny Randall, hostess. Nine rooms, several with private bath. Rates: $50 to $125. Includes continental breakfast. Children over ten; no pets; Visa/MasterCard/American Express. Smoking permitted in porch areas.

DIRECTIONS: from L.A. take 405 to Washington Street and make a right heading towards the ocean. Turn right at Speedway and the house is on the right corner. Parking in the rear. Ten minutes from LAX.

CROWN BED & BREAKFAST

A classic example of the Craftsman style

Designed and built single-handedly in 1905 by Louis B. Easton, who lived next door, this house was created in the spirit of the Arts and Crafts movement. It is a strong statement against mass production and conformity and presents a classic example of the Craftsman style of architecture, featuring hand-hewn wooden interiors and hand-forged metalwork. It is dedicated to a pure aesthetic and functional simplicity.

After being restored by the Pasadena Heritage from original drawings, the building was sold to a group who assumed stewardship of the historic house. Two purposes were served: the society used the money it realized to restore a second building in Pasadena; and Pasadena's first bed and breakfast was born.

Guest rooms are spacious enough to offer seating areas with comfortable chairs, and several of the rooms have couches that make up into a double bed. Rattan furniture reminiscent of the period and special pieces re-created from Louis B. Easton designs comprise most of the furnishings.

Greeted by hostess Nancy Arnold, a visitor will find this a comfortable lodging alternative while attending the Rose Bowl, visiting the civic center and Norton Simon Museum, or enjoying the renaissance of Pasadena's restaurants. Niceties at the Crown include a glass of wine upon arrival, chilled fruit and flowers in rooms.

CROWN BED & BREAKFAST INN , 530 S. Marengo Ave., Pasadena, CA 91101; (818) 792-4031; Nancy Arnold, hostess. Five rooms, four with private baths. Rates: $80 double occupancy. Includes well presented continental breakfast. Well-behaved children over twelve; no pets; smoking in downstairs common areas only; American Express.

DIRECTIONS: from L.A./Pasadena Freeway, exit 11 becomes Arroya Parkway. Make a right onto California St. and a left onto Marengo.

Left, the house's fine cabinetry exemplifies the best of the Arts and Crafts movement at the turn-of-the-century. Above, copies of Stickley furniture flank the clinker-brick fireplace.

THE LEMON TREE

Refreshing scents and fragrances

Beautifully situated amidst the lemon groves and avocado trees of Santa Paula, the citrus capital of the world, the Lemon Tree was once the center of a twelve-hundred-acre ranch. In addition to lemon trees and avocados, there are twenty varieties of fruit trees here, including persimmon, peach, kiwi, pear, and plum

An elegant rose garden surrounds the house and a miniature boxwood hedge frames a flower bed thick with a rainbow of poppies. The secluded jasmine-covered brick patio is a favorite spot among guests. Three glass-covered wrought iron tables with bright yellow and white cushioned chairs make the patio delightful for morning coffee.

During the day, when the Victorian farmhouse is filled with sunshine, expansive picture windows in the library, dining room, and parlor give the feeling of being outdoors among the camelia bushes and flowers. At dusk, a dozen yellow and gold, lemon-scented candles sparkle in the parlor's corner, where guests gather to taste wine and to enjoy tangy guacamole, a house specialty.

The rooms are bright and airy. Helen's Room in lavender, pink, and white has lots of lacy pillows, while Bess's Room in blue with white wicker furniture overlooks the orchards and the mountains. Carrie's Room, a cheerful buttercup yellow, has a hand-crocheted comforter and patchwork quilt. Two gold velvet arm chairs and a vanity with a tall mirror reflect the soft glow.

Sally and Phil Snow are relaxed and pleasing hosts. Guests leave this quiet country retreat feeling refreshed by their hospitality.

THE LEMON TREE, 299 West Santa Paula Street, Santa Paula, CA 93060; (805) 525-7747; Phil & Sally Snow, hosts. Four rooms; two with private bath, two share one large sunlit bath. Rates $55 to $65. Includes a lovely breakfast of fresh fruits and breads served either in the sunny dining room or outside on the covered patio. No smoking, children, or pets. Visa/MasterCard.

DIRECTIONS: from the south, take Santa Paula Freeway exit 126 onto Palm Avenue and make a right. Proceed to West Santa Paula Street and make a left. Follow the numbers to 299 and the white mailbox will be on the right. From the north, exit 126 at Peck Road and make a left. Proceed to Santa Paula Street and make a right. The Inn is less than a mile on the left just past Armore Street.

Wooden sculpture by Boyd Wright.

OJAI MANOR HOTEL

An artistic approach

Innkeeper Mary Nelson's stylish good taste and the exciting sculpture created by her partner, Boyd Wright, harmonize perfectly at the Ojai Manor. The place is immediately engaging because of the very personal combination of fine, traditional turn-of-the-century furnishings with modern prints, collages, and paintings by friends and associates.

Built in 1874, the manor is reported to be the oldest building in Ojai and served the "heart and soul" of the community as a schoolhouse, town hall, and hotel before it was bought in the 1950s by Mary's family. Just one block from the town's main street and a few blocks from a wonderful outdoor used bookstore and several highly recommended restaurants, the manor attracts low-keyed travelers who come here to relax and do little else, which is not to imply that the more active will find little to do. Mary recommends a trip up to Wheeler's Hot Springs for the massages and mineral baths, or a walk over to Libby Park during the jazz and classical music festivals.

In the evening, guests can sink into deep blue-velvet couches next to the fireplace and have a glass of sherry. Or they can pull up a big willow chair near the pot-bellied stove in the dining room. Whatever they do, they will be surrounded by the great variety of original artworks that make the manor special.

OJAI MANOR HOTEL, 210 East Matilija, Ojai, CA 93023; (805) 646-0961; Mary Nelson, host. Six tastefully appointed rooms that share three baths. Rates $65 to $75. Includes buffet continental breakfast of fresh fruits and fresh baking, such as cinnamon rolls or apple strudels. Children over 12; no smoking; pets negotiable. A bit of Spanish spoken. Visa/MasterCard.

DIRECTIONS: from U.S.-101 take Rte. 33 for 14 miles to Ojai exit. After the first stoplight in Ojai go one mile to second light and turn left onto Signal Street. One block to Matilija Street and turn right.

Mission bed from a small Western hotel.

Left, a handsome live oak tree contrasts with the clean lines of the house.

ROSEHOLM

Sound of Vivaldi; scent of roses

Perched on a hill just southwest of Ojai, this rose-colored Mediterranean villa resembles a fairy-tale castle. Set behind black wrought iron gates, it is reached by a short uphill drive. The sound of water rushing from four lion-headed fountains, the strains of Vivaldi, the scent and shade of the Cecil Bruner rose-covered arbor, the high vine-covered courtyard wall, help to shelter guests from the outside world.

Stepping through the arched doorway of Roseholm, one is engulfed in luxury. Beautiful furnishings delight the eye; vases of long stemmed roses are everywhere—lemon, lavender, salmon—their scent permeating the entire house. Although expensive, Roseholm is not pretentiously opulent. Miraculously, it maintains a carefree, understated elegance.

Host and hostess Jan and Patti Harmonson, appear casual as they greet guests in matching pink polo shirts embroidered with the Roseholm emblem. Behind this informality is the self-assurance of knowing that everything is perfect—from the champagne to the gourmet treats awaiting the guests. Prepared under the supervision of a renowned chef, one may be treated to a breakfast of eggs Benedict with tender asparagus, lobster or shrimp wrapped in filo for tea, or a luscious chocolate mousse cake for evening dessert. The wine cellar is open for guests to taste and select wines of their liking.

Each cottage and room is named for a type of rose: Tiffany, Masquerade, Bewitched, Paradise. The Masquerade room has an oval mirror over a marble fireplace, elegantly upholstered chairs, a spacious white tiled bathroom, and a bank of eleven windows with a glorious view.

Several cottages have private Jacuzzis and for more socially-minded guests there is a large Jacuzzi in the courtyard that can accommodate six. A cozy library with high-back red leather chairs and the air of a private club welcomes those who wish to relax indoors. Guests adore the quiet elegance that Roseholm offers.

Each suite has its own Jacuzzi.

ROSEHOLM, 51 Sulphur Mountain Road, Ventura, CA 93001; (805) 649-4014; Patti & Jan Harmonson, hosts. Four rooms in the main house, all with private baths. Several separate cottages. Rates: main house $215 to $296. Guest Houses: $245 to $570. Most with indoor or outdoor Jacuzzis and fireplaces. Includes gourmet high tea, after-dinner desserts and full breakfast. Open Wine Cellar. Music is piped into each room. Smoking outdoors.

DIRECTIONS: provided at the time of reservation. Halfway between Ventura and Ojai.

Nesting quail in front of the Wood Thrush Cottage.

BLUE QUAIL INN

Guest rooms named after birds

Country charm, piping hot popovers, and picnic lunches to take along on bike rides await guests at Jeanise Suding's Blue Quail Inn. Although Santa Barbara can be stylish and chic, this inn suits those who are looking for straightforward comfort.

The style of this complex, consisting of a main house and four cottages, is very contemporary, and Jeanise has decorated the rooms with big, beautiful country quilts, porcelain farm animals, canopied beds, and overstuffed chairs. A choice of guest rooms includes the Whippoorwill, the Meadowlark, the Wood Thrush, and the Nightingale, as well as five other rooms also named after birds.

There is plenty of yard surrounding the cottages,

and guests can lounge outside when they are not indulging in Santa Barbara's seashore or attractive shops. Breakfast is served on a big old country-pine farm table, and the smell of hot cider, apple muffins and persimmon bread fills the house.

BLUE QUAIL INN, 1908 Bath Street, Santa Barbara, CA 93101; (805) 687-2300. Jeanise Suding, hostess. Eight rooms in main house and four cottages, six with private baths. Rates: $45 to $75 winter; $60 to $85 summer. Children over twelve; no pets; smoking preferred outside; Visa/MasterCard.

DIRECTIONS: US-101 south, exit at Mission Street offramp and turn left. Proceed one block and turn right onto Castillo Street. In one block turn left onto Pedregosa Street. Proceed one block and turn left onto Bath Street. US-101 north, take the Arrellaga Street offramp. Proceed two blocks and turn left onto Bath Street.

Hostess Jeanise Suding and friend Rodney.

THE PARSONAGE

The European tradition

Hilde Michelmore's energy, style, and warmth are evident the moment you step through the door of the Parsonage. This 1892 Queen Anne house is filled with the ebullient personality of its hostess. Raised in Europe, with its tradition of hospitality, Hilde receives guests graciously and makes their visits memorable. All comes effortlessly, whether she is serving a lavish breakfast of French toast or apple pancakes, sharing the afternoon cocktail hour, or helping someone plan an evening.

In the living room, an emerald green and deep purple Oriental carpet serves as a vibrant backdrop for the antiques and original redwood trim that are stylishly combined with modern furnishings.

Upstairs, the Las Flores room, with its unusual marble-topped sideboard and antique armoire, recaptures the era when this building was a rectory.

Mirrored bedroom set in the Honeymoon Suite.

The spacious outdoor deck is made for sun worshipers, and it is easy to curl up in one of the lounge chairs with a good book. Breakfast is often served at one of the umbrella-covered tables, and if light exercise is in order, the famous mission is a short and pleasant walk away.

THE PARSONAGE, 1600 Olive Street, Santa Barbara, CA 93101; (805) 962-9336; Hilde Michelmore, hostess. Fluent in German. Six rooms, each with private bath. Rates: $65 to $110. Includes full, delicious breakfast. Children over fourteen welcome; no pets; smoking allowed. Beautiful pearl-grey cat in residence.

DIRECTIONS: from the south on US-101, exit onto State Street. Follow State and take a right onto Arrellaga Street. Proceed to Olive Street and the house is on the corner. From the north on US-101, exit onto Mission Street. Go to end of Mission and make right onto Laguna for 1 block and left onto Olive.

Hostess Hilde Michelmore and her Russian blue cat.

Alice's Room

THE CHESHIRE CAT

Alice in Ashleyland

Lewis Carroll would be delighted with the wonderland created at The Cheshire Cat, two beige and white Victorian houses in the heart of residential Santa Barbara. Meticulously landscaped grounds are enhanced by a high peaked, white lattice gazebo. White porch railings and columns, white lace curtains in the windows, and white trim on the houses give The Cheshire Cat a polished look.

Each room is its own Lewis Carroll fantasy. Laura Ashley draperies, bedspreads, chair fabrics, and wallpapers are carefully coordinated in color and pattern. Even the lamp shades are covered in fabric; sapphire and white in The Mock Turtle chamber, plum and cream in The Mad Hatter. The rooms have a precious but romantic flair. The carpeting is plush, the satin comforters alluring.

Breakfast is served in the comfortable country-style dining room or on the brick patio, and fine English china patterned with small strawberries adds a touch of elegance to the continental fare. Baileys Bristol Cream awaits week-end guests upon arrival as does a box of chocolates from Santa Barbara's famous Chocolate Box. The large grey "all seeing cat" adds to the fantasy.

THE CHESHIRE CAT, 36 West Valerio Street, Santa Barbara, CA 93101; (805) 569-1610; Chris Dunstan, host. Ten rooms in two adjacent houses, all with private baths; one with blue-tiled Jacuzzi in the room, one with fireplace, and several with patios. Rates: $99 to $139. Includes continental breakfast served on outdoor patio or in dining room. No children, smoking, or pets. No credit cards.

DIRECTIONS: from the south on US-101, at Arellaga exit, take a right. Proceed on Arellaga and make a left onto Chapala. Go 1–2 block to Vallerio; the inn is on the corner. From the north on US-101, take the Mission Street exit. Take a left on De La Vina, a left on Valerio and proceed 2 blocks.

THE TIFFANY INN

Exquisite antiques

Within walking distance of shops, restaurants, and theaters, and only half a mile to the beach, The Tiffany Inn is situated in the heart of downtown Santa Barbara.

The MacDonalds have placed extraordinarily fine pieces throughout the house. Antiques range from formal, such as the elaborately carved Victorian Renaissance bed and armoire in the Somerset Room, to the casual country oak of the Rose Garden Room. The velvet puff sleeved drapery, the white lace curtains, and the beautifully upholstered chairs reflect the meticulous care and straightforward elegance that typifies this inn. The restoration of this stately mansion was clearly a labor of love for Carol and Larry.

THE TIFFANY INN, 1323 De La Vina, Santa Barbara, CA 93101; (805) 963-2283; Carol & Larry MacDonald, hosts. Five rooms, three with private baths, several with fireplaces. Rates: $75 to $110. Includes expanded continental breakfast and evening wine and hors d'oeuvres. Children over 12; smoking on patio; off-street parking. Visa/MasterCard. Inquire about mid-season and corporate rates.

DIRECTIONS: from the south on US-101, exit at State Street and go right (north) onto State. Proceed 9 blocks and turn left onto Sola. Go 2 blocks and turn left onto De La Vina. From the north on US-101, exit at Mission Street and turn left (east) onto Mission. Proceed for 3 blocks and make a right onto De La Vina.

The Somerset Room has this handsome Renaissance bed.

RED ROSE INN

Delightful Victorian in Santa Barbara

Chosen by the Santa Barbara Historical Society to be featured in *Survivors*, a publication recording the city's finest examples of Victorian architecture, this inn is a delight. There is a crisp, coordinated charm to the place that reflects the fresh and youthful personalities of its hosts, Neile Ifland, who likes to bake, and Rick Ifland, a serious runner. Owners of a tandem bike, they insist it is the only way to see the town or beach, especially with the picnic lunches that Neile loves to pack.

There is something in every corner of the house to evoke a smile: a stained-glass window, a bed with a direct provenance to Abraham Lincoln, and a framed ladies' fan that doubles as an 1897 calendar, with a blond cherub decorating each of the months.

A portrait of a woman hangs in each of the guest rooms, and although they are not famous opera singers or infamous women of the Wild West, they are held in high esteem. This is not surprising for they are Neile and Rick's great grandmothers, whose presence reflects the warm sentiment you find here.

RED ROSE INN, 1416 Castillo, Santa Barbara, CA 93101; (805) 966-1470; Neile and Rick Ifland, hosts. Four rooms, two with private bath. Rates: $55 to $75 double. No children; no pets; smoking outside only; Visa/MasterCard.

DIRECTIONS: from US-101, exit onto Arrellaga Street. Proceed to Castillo Street one block east.

Sunset signals the time for wine and cheese at the Red Rose.

THE BAYBERRY INN

New England opulence

"I want my guests to feel as if they are returning to visit a well-to-do grandma," comments Carlton Wagner of Carlton Wagner Designs. He and Keith Pomeroy, who has a background in catering, have combined their talents to provide a gracious in-town bed and breakfast. No detail is too insignificant, no decoration too extravagant for this ambitious showcase restoration. The owners have been successful in achieving an opulence undreamed of by grandma.

Seventeenth-century Italian walnut chairs covered with flambovant tapestry surround the apricot marble dining table. A grand piano entices those who are musically inclined, and a dozen or so candles on the living room mantel set a luxurious mood. Guest rooms are named and color coordinated for different berries. The Blueberry Room has its own sun room and all rooms have canopied beds.

The transition from the house to the large yard is heralded by the sweet sound of zebra finches chirping on the sun porch. Once outside, classical sculpture, a gazebo, and a recessed Victorian lattice for plantings offer an elegant outdoor retreat.

THE BAYBERRY INN, 111 West Valerio Street, Santa Barbara, CA 93101; (805) 682-3199; Carlton Wagner and Keith Pomeroy, hosts. Eight rooms, all with private baths; four with fireplaces. Rates: $75 to $125. Includes a full breakfast with gourmet egg dish. Children over twelve; no pets; smoking on outside deck; Visa/MasterCard/American Express. Two terriers in residence.

DIRECTIONS: from the south via US-101: after passing the State Street exit, go one block and turn right onto Chapalla. Continue 13 blocks to Valerio Street and the inn is on the left corner. From the north via US-101: at the Mission Street exit, take a left onto Mission Street and a right onto De La Vina. Continue on De La Vina and take a left onto Valerio Street. The Inn is one block on the right.

The Strawberry Room.

The Sun Porch bathroom for the Blueberry Room.

Left, the newly decorated dining room.

Left, four shades of rose grace the restored building. A multitude of windows illuminate the rooms, as in the one above.

ROSE VICTORIAN INN

Spectacular inside and out

This 1885 landmark home, once surrounded by walnut tree farms, continues to dominate the horizon of the farmlands of San Luis Obispo County. Painted in four shades of rose, it rises toward the sky, a majestic fifty-five-foot four-story Victorian.

The inn has become a romantic mecca. More than one hundred brides have walked along the thirty-foot rose arbor to the gazebo to meet their grooms. Celebrating anniversaries at the Rose Victorian is a tradition many couples still honor.

The appeal of the Rose Victorian goes far beyond its imposing stature, given the warmth and whimsy of the Cox family. Enthusiastic, cheerful, and downright hospitable, this family sees to it that guests are comfortable and enjoy themselves. Champagne contributes to conviviality at breakfast, and accompanies a feast of eggs Benedict, artfully prepared by Shelly, and ham-and-cheese or nut-and-raisin stuffed croissants. For the guest on a modified American plan, dinner is included in the room tariff, and the varied, high-quality menu, courteous service, and lovely dining room reflect the Coxes' credo that dining be a fine experience. It is not surprising that the Rose Victorian offers the best dining in the area.

For guests who like to pass a quiet evening, there is a large parlor perfect for deliberating over a jigsaw puzzle or for playing an especially beautiful 1875 rosewood square grand piano. The nearby Great American Melodrama and Vaudeville show is recommended for those who like to hiss and boo at the villain.

ROSE VICTORIAN INN, 789 Valley Road, Arroyo Grande, CA 93420; (805) 481-5566; Diana and Ross Cox, owners. Eight rooms, three with private bath; remaining five rooms share three baths. Each room decorated in keeping with Victorian period. Rates: $105 to $120 modified American plan with full breakfast and six course dinner for two. Children over sixteen; no pets; smoking in the restaurant and gardens, but not in the house. Collie, Australian shepherd, and three entertaining cats in residence.

DIRECTIONS: located 200 miles north of L.A. and 250 miles south of San Francisco. Take Traffic Way exit from US-101. Turn left at the stop sign onto Fair Oaks, go ¼ mile and turn left onto Valley Road. Proceed ¼ mile to the inn.

Chef Clifford Replogle's morning buffet.

THE BALLARD INN

Celebrates the past

"The Ballard Inn believes in courtship and reverie, dreams and flights of fancy. We dedicate this room to Cynthia and all the pioneer women who triumphed over hardship and believed in enduring romance of life."

The tone of the inn is commemorative. Vintage photographs and memorabilia decorate each room of the inn and depict persons, events, or themes important to the heritage of the San Ynez Valley. Researched and decorated by Catherine Kaufman, a Los Angeles designer, each room is unique. In the room honoring early settler and trapper Davy Brown, a fireplace built with stones from the San Ynez River, a distressed oak floor, and a wagon-wheel quilt simulate the interior of an authentic log cabin. In contrast, the Wildflower Room, which highlights native flowers, is as sweet and lovely as its name implies. Decorated in lavender, pink, and coral, it has a Bloomsbury quilt and gentle sewing rocker. The Equestrian Room is outfitted to celebrate a rich history of horse breeding in the valley. The Jarado Room pays tribute to the native Chumash Indian with designs and colors inspired by red, black, and white cave paintings found in the area.

The inn and its cuisine may be described in one word—expansive. Guests may "design" their own multiple course breakfast from a buffet of fruits, cheeses, breads, and a choice among three or four splendid entrées. There are several common rooms, including a den with a VCR and a large living room where one may enjoy a sumptuous afternoon buffet of cheeses and pastries.

The San Ynez Valley is a special place. Twelve wineries are within close proximity of the Ballard Inn. Large ranches and several world class Arabian horse breeders are also nearby. Home of many theater and movie personalities, a strong tradition of good taste and style pervades this valley. Beth, the energetic and enthusiastic innkeeper, sees to it that her guests are treated with that same spirit.

THE BALLARD INN, 2436 Baseline, Ballard, CA 93463; (805) 688-7770; Beth Bryan, host. Fifteen rooms, all with private baths, several with fireplaces. Rates: $120 to $150. Includes afternoon refreshments, cheeses, and hors d'ouerves and incredible breakfast that just won't quit. Dutch, German and some French is spoken. Handicap access. Visa/MasterCard.

DIRECTIONS: from the north take US-101, to Rte. 154 to Los Olivos; turn south (right) on Alamo Pintado Road towards Ballard. From the south take US-101 to Rte. 246, through Solvang. Go north (left) on Alamo Pintado Road.

J. PATRICK HOUSE

Nestled into the pines

Innkeeper Molly Lynch laughingly notes, "Having an inn was a fantasy, pure and clear." Now she offers visitors a place to relax and enjoy themselves. And indeed, a log cabin amidst the pine covered hills of Cambria—the J. Patrick House—fills the bill. Rough-hewn logs, a cuddly pooh bear plunked in a rocking chair by the fireside, and a kitchen filled with hanging copper pots create a casual, homey mood.

The guest rooms, named after Irish counties like Kerry and Limerick, are in an adjacent two-story building connected to the log house by a long arbor entwined with flame-red passion vines.

With the inn just six miles from Hearst Castle, visiting San Simeon is a favorite outing for many of Molly's guests. Others enjoy touring the nearby vineyards, going to the beach, or browsing through the delightful little shops in Cambria. After busy days, guests look forward to relaxing by the fireside in the early evening with wine and cheese.

A framed embroidery from 1934 reads: "Guest, you are welcome here, be at your ease. Get up when you're ready, go to bed when you please. Happy to share with you such as we've got, the leaks in the roof, the soup in the pot. You don't have to thank us or laugh at our jokes. Sit deep and come often, you're one of the folks."

J. PATRICK HOUSE, 2990 Burton Drive, Cambria, CA 93428; (805) 927-3812; Molly Lynch, host. Seven rooms, each with private bath and fireplace. Rates: $80. Includes evening refreshments and extended continental breakfast such as fruit, yogurt, cinnamon rolls. No smoking, children, or pets; Visa/MasterCard. Mid-way between LA and San Francisco.

DIRECTIONS: from the south take US-101. Ignore first Cambria exit, then exit at Burton Drive and turn right. The house is ¼ mile on the right. From the north take US-101 and exit at Burton Drive and turn left.

MONTEREY

THE JABBERWOCK

Enjoy a breakfast of Razzleberries

Named after the mythical character in Lewis Carroll's poem "Jabberwocky," this Jabberwock is a special bed and breakfast where two themes prevail. First, there is humor in everything that hosts Jim and Barbara Allen undertake. From the presentation of a tantalizing series of mysterious hors d'oeuvres at aperitif hour to the surprise breakfast, everything is a curiosity. Anything from Snarkleberry, Razzleberry, or Frabjous may appear on the menu. The guest rooms have names too: Tulgey Wood, Mome Rath, or Brillig.

The second prevailing theme at the Jabberwock is hospitality, a flair for which Barbara developed during thirteen years spent in the hotel industry. Everything is first quality here, from the lace-trimmed sheets to the special down comforters.

Details have been carefully attended to, such as writing first names of guests on a chalkboard, or leaving binoculars on windowsills for a bay view. Jim, a recently retired captain of the Los Angeles Fire Department, has his own style and penchant for fun, and it is well worth asking him for a tour in the British Beardmore taxi.

Once a convent, the Jabberwock makes a large, elegant home. The living room is luxurious, and the wraparound sun porch is especially inviting. Gardens and a waterfall only enhance what Jim and Barbara have created to make your visit to the Monterey Peninsula memorable.

THE JABBERWOCK, 598 Laine Street, Monterey, CA 93940; (408) 372-4777; Jim and Barbara Allen, hosts. Barbara speaks French, Danish, and Spanish. Seven rooms, three with private baths. Rates: $75 to $140. Includes imaginative, delicious breakfast, a delectable selection of hors d'oeuvres and warm cookies and milk before bed. No children; no pets; no smoking except on the sun porch; no credit cards. Popular English bull terrier in residence. Four blocks above Cannery Row and Monterey Bay aquarium.

DIRECTIONS: from Rte. 1 take Rte. 68 west for 2½ miles. Turn right onto Prescott and right onto Pine for one block and then turn left onto Hoffman. The Jabberwock is on the corner of Hoffman and Laine.

Special treats await guests at bed-time.

Guests in this room are enthralled by the view.

MARTINE INN

Ocean front villa

The luxury and beauty of the Monterey Peninsula can be found at this pink stucco Mediterranean style villa. The coastline is at the doorstep and the windows of the inn afford sweeping vistas for watching whales, sea otters, sailboat races, and crashing waves. Most of the rooms have an ocean view, but for those without that privilege, there are sitting rooms on each floor with a panoramic view.

For furnishing each guest room the Martines have selected a particular period or style and furnished them with the most remarkable pieces available. A Chinese wedding bed with dozens of hand-painted panels, a formal mahogany bedroom set featured at the 1869 World's Fair, and an art deco room complete with lit Coca-Cola sign, are examples of the scope and depth of the décor. In the American Room there is a rare American armoire dating back to 1850 with a cherry wood interior and bird's eye maple surface. Two Victorian tobacco stands with copper lined humidors serve as end tables. In another room a Captain's bed is ornamented with carved ship's wheels.

Since the days when it was home to Laura and James Parke of Parke-Davis Pharmaceuticals, gala entertaining of socialites and dignitaries has been part of the Martine Inn. The same grandeur prevails today as Marion Martine explains: "We are entertaining the same way today they would have at the turn of the century."

All of the exquisite silver and furnishings throughout the house are of museum quality. Quite impressive is the immense Sheffield silver server made in 1765 and graciously incorporated into the breakfast presentation. Adding further elegance is a rare globe-shaped Victorian reposse silver butter dish, silver coffee and tea service, and elegant Syracuse china.

MARTINE INN, 255 Ocean View Boulevard, Pacific Grove, CA 93950; (408) 373-3388; Marion & Don Martine, hosts. Nineteen elegantly furnished rooms, each with private bath; several with fireplaces, several with ocean view. Rates: $85 to $165. Includes full gourmet breakfast served in dining room with spectacular view. Hors d'ouevres and refreshments in the evening. Antique silver service used for coffee and teas. Golf, tennis, jogging path, bike path all adjacent or nearby. Four blocks from Monterey Peninsula Aquarium & Cannery Row. German, Spanish, and Italian spoken. No children; handicap access; Visa/MasterCard/American Express.

DIRECTIONS: from Rte. 1, take Pacific Grove/Pebble Beach exit. Follow signs to Pacific Grove. Proceed on Rte. 68, which becomes Forrest Avenue, and follow all the way to Ocean View Blvd. Take a right and go 10 blocks to the inn.

SEVEN GABLES INN

Museum-quality opulence

Filled with an impressive collection of fine art, statuary, ornamental china, and antique furnishings, the House of the Seven Gables is one of the grandest homes on the Monterey Peninsula. The result of thoughtful choices made over many decades, it is filled with pieces acquired by John and Nora Flatley during their extensive travels. Not bought to be coveted as "museum pieces," the extravagant collection is used and enjoyed by family and guests.

Whether you are discovering an eighteenth-century oil painting or marveling at the detailing on a Sèvres vase, the hosts are delighted you noticed. Six family members, who share various aspects of innkeeping, will be happy to tell you an interesting aside about a particular marble statue or piece of ornate furniture. Notice the beautiful sunset if you happen to be in the dining room. The rays bounce off a monumental crystal chandelier and reflect in a floor-to-ceiling pier mirror.

Since they became innkeepers in 1958, the Flatleys have lovingly tended the flower gardens that border their house and the imposing shoreline. Lovers' Point Beach and the sea are just steps away, and the dramatic Monterey coastline can be seen from each of the inn's twelve guest rooms. Cannery Row is a three-minute drive or a short walk along the waterfront, and the famous Seventeen-Mile Drive begins at the front door.

SEVEN GABLES INN, 555 Ocean View Boulevard, Pacific Grove, CA 93950; (408) 372-4341; John and Nora Flatley and family, owners. Susan, Fred, Ed, and Heather are adult family members involved with the various facets of innkeeping. Spanish, French, and Arabic spoken. Fourteen rooms in the main house and in several separate cottages and a carriage house, all with full baths. Rates: $85 to $135. Includes continental breakfast that often offers scones or, on summer Sundays, strawberry shortcake. Children over twelve; no pets; no smoking; personal checks accepted; afternoon tea served. Cats Al and Whisper.

DIRECTIONS: from Rte. 1 north take Pacific Grove-Del Monte exit. Take Del Monte (which becomes Lighthouse Ave.) through the tunnel and into Pacific Grove. Go right one block to Ocean View Blvd., then left to Fountain Ave. and the inn. From Rte. 1 south take Pacific Grove-Pebble Beach Exit. Once in Pacific Grove take Forest Ave. to Ocean View Blvd., and then right two blocks to Fountain Ave. and the inn.

Left, the house contains a collection of extraordinary antiques.

THE SEA VIEW

Sixty years of hospitality

The broad white sand beaches of the Pacific are a stone's throw from the Sea View Inn's front porch. This three-story, wood-shingle, Craftsman bungalow was built in 1910 and has served as an inn for more than sixty years. Decorated with an eclectic mix of period pieces, the overall atmosphere is relaxed and comfortable.

The house sits on one of the quiet byways that crisscross Carmel. These tree-shaded lanes, free of streetlamps and concrete walks, preserve a rustic charm that nurtures gentle spirits.

The inn is close to Point Lobos, the Carmel mission, and the famous Pebble Beach golf course.

THE SEA VIEW, between 11th and 12th on Camino Real, P.O. Box 4138, Carmel, CA 93921; (408) 624-8778; Marshall and Diane Hydorn, owners; Brenda Starr, manager. Some French spoken. Eight rooms, six with private baths. Rates: $57 to $88. Includes buffet-style breakfast of cereals, pastries, and non-sweet breads; egg dish on Sundays. No children under twelve; no pets; smoking on outside porch where ashtrays and chairs are provided; Visa/MasterCard.

DIRECTIONS: take Ocean Ave. exit off Rte. 1 and proceed on Ocean. Turn left onto Camino Real and proceed 5½ blocks to inn.

Hosts Marshal and Diane Hydorn and their 1910 Bungalow.

Owner and host Dr. Joe Megna greets guests in the lobby.

THE CENTRELLA

A million-dollar revival

Touted by journalists at the turn-of-the-century as "the largest, most commodious, and pleasantly located private boarding house in the Grove," the Centrella is now experiencing a revival. The entirely refurbished million dollar interior, replete with wainscoted hallways, stained-glass and beveled windows, antique furniture, and electrified gas fixtures, has received the Gold Key Award for "excellence in guest room interior."

A large common room with a marble-faced fireplace serves as a gathering place for guests in the evening as well as for buffet breakfasts that include pastries, fruit, and yogurt. Turrets, bay windows, gingerbread, and graceful porches add to the attractiveness of this vintage hotel. In addition to rooms in the main building, there are five separate cottages with fireplaces, refrigerators, and sitting areas.

Located in the heart of Pacific Grove amid old Victorian homes and redwood trees, the Centrella is a block-and-a-half from the ocean and Lovers' Point. It is a three-minute drive from the soon-to-be-completed, eagerly awaited aquarium.

THE CENTRELLA, 612 Central Avenue, P.O. Box 51157, Pacific Grove, CA 93950; (408) 372-3372; Joe and Florence Megna, innkeepers. Fluent Italian. Twenty-six rooms, which includes eighteen individual rooms, two honeymoon attic suites, and five separate cottages with fireplaces, refrigerators, and sitting areas. Rates: $65 to $150 double. Includes continental breakfast of pastries and fresh fruit, yogurt, and bran and a light repast at Social Hour. Children over twelve in main house; any age in separate cottages; smoking permitted in rooms but not in public areas; wheelchair access to rooms on ground floor; Visa/MasterCard, American Express.

DIRECTIONS: Rte. 1 to Pacific Grove exit, which is Rte. 68.

CHÂTEAU VICTORIAN

Colorful Victorian

One block from the newly renovated Santa Cruz boardwalk, Château Victorian offers a pleasing array of accommodations. Several of the seven bedrooms contain working fireplaces, and all have modern private baths, a sitting area, and a tasteful selection of antique furnishings. For sun-worshipers the inn provides a large brick courtyard, and a wooden deck at the front of the house faces the shoreline bustle.

The boardwalk, painted in brilliant rainbow hues, exudes a magnetic and lively carnival air. Amid an atmosphere filled with the aroma of popcorn, hot dogs, and cotton candy, visitors can ride the roller coaster or play games of chance in the penny arcade.

CHÂTEAU VICTORIAN, 118 First Street, Santa Cruz, CA 95060; (408) 458-9458; Franz and Alice-June Benjamin, hosts. German spoken. Seven rooms, each with private bath. Rates: $70 to $100. Includes buffet breakfast of croissants, fruit platters, afternoon and evening refreshments. No children; no pets; no smoking; all major credit cards.

DIRECTIONS: Rte. 17 into Santa Cruz, which becomes Ocean St. Follow to the end and take a right onto San Lorenzo Blvd. Proceed three blocks to first traffic light and take a left onto Riverside St. Cross over bridge and turn right onto Second St., left onto Cliff St., and right onto First St.

Ancestral portraits enliven the dining room.

Left, the entrance hall to a splendid Victorian parlor. Above, the Orchard Room, aptly named for its view of the surrounding orchards.

APPLE LANE INN

Enchanting Victorian décor

*A life without festivity
is like a road without an Inn.*
—Democratus (450 B.C.)

Once surrounded by sixty acres of apple orchards, this 1876 Victorian farmhouse retains the flavor of its original setting. Approached along a lane lined with apple trees and an old barn, the view opens onto a quiet patio with a grape arbor and lots of wonderful bright flowers.

All the enchantment of Victorian décor is displayed here, from the mahogany furniture and Oriental rugs in the formal parlor to the bedrooms on the second floor. On the third floor, Victorian conventions give way to an airy country style, where colorful stencils decorate floors, walls, and window shades. Dhurrie rugs with pastel accents combine cheerfully with white walls, painted rafters, and a pitched roof.

Small touches add to the pleasing quality of Apple Lane, such as the polished fresh apples tucked beside each guest's pillow. A collection of antique dolls embellishes one room, and in another a high four-poster bed carved with pineapples symbolizes the hospitality so apparent throughout the inn.

There are books everywhere and lots of wonderful art, from black and white photgraphs by Ansel Adams and Carleton Watkins, to Oriental rubbings and contemporary oils. Rare maps are beautifully displayed, revealing the host's scholarly interest in geography.

APPLE LANE INN, 6265 Soquel Drive, Aptos, CA 95003; (408) 475-6868; Barbara Buckmaster and Peter Farqhuar, owners. Five rooms, with private and shared baths. Rates: $65 to $95. Inquire about discounts during the week. Includes a full breakfast. Children over twelve; no pets; smoking in the parlors only; Visa/MasterCard/American Express.

DIRECTIONS: from Rte. 1 north, exit at Seacliff Beach and turn right on four-way stop. Take a left onto Soquel Drive. Proceed slightly over a mile, and just past Cabrillo College look carefully on the right for a sign to Apple Lane. From Rte. 1 south turn left onto Park Avenue and right onto Soquel Ave. Look for a sign on the left just before Cabrillo College.

THE MANGELS HOUSE

Antebellum mansion

The dramatic approach along the winding road of Nisene Park indicates that this bed and breakfast is going to be special. Framed by a white picket fence, the Mangels House sits high atop a long driveway. A century-old palm tree stands sentinel in the circular drive.

The stately symmetry of the architecture, a wrap around columned porch, tall windows, and a broad stairway to a double door entrance are impressive. Built as a rural vacation home in 1886 by Claus Mangels, brother-in-law of sugar baron Claus Spreckels, the Southern style mansion is the epitome of grace and charm, down to the white fringed porch swing and wisteria ascending the porch's columns.

Jackie, the English born innkeeper, has a marvelously fresh contemporary taste, blending modern art and country Victorian décor. The living room is so enormous that it dwarfs a grand piano. An eight foot wide floor-to-ceiling rough-cut marble fireplace with its three foot logs increases the imposing scale.

Mangels' lemon-hued dining room is similarly grand, its sparse majesty enhanced by a long narrow table, polished to a high gloss. The only adornment is a formal portrait of Claus Mangels behind the head of the table and portraits of his two wives on either side of the room. Because the ceilings are high, the straight staircase just inside the entry rises with dramatic elegance to the second floor bedrooms.

THE MANGELS HOUSE, 570 Aptos Creek Road, P.O. Box 302, Aptos, CA 95001; (408) 688-7982; Jacqueline and Ron Fisher, hosts. Five rooms, two with private baths. Rates: $78 to $96. Includes breakfast of fruits and breads and often an herb omelet. Spanish and French spoken. Smoking in sitting room and on porches. Children over 12; Visa/MasterCard.

DIRECTIONS: from Rte. 1 take Seacliff Beach/Aptos exit. Turn onto Sequel Drive. Proceed ⅓ mile under the RR Bridge. About 100 feet on the left, before the shopping center, take a left onto Aptos Creek Road. Follow along winding road for ½ mile; the sign and house are on the right.

The Mauve Room has a marble fireplace.

Breakfast becomes an extraordinary experience in this room.

CLIFF CREST

Breakfasting with Mozart and Brahms

This sprightly Queen Anne is tucked into the historic area of Beach Hill, a surprisingly quiet residential community. Near the beach, boardwalk, and fisherman's wharf, it was built in 1890 for a lieutenant governor of California who helped to establish Redwoods State Park.

The most dramatic feature of the house is a two-story belvedere tower. The ground floor of the tower, where breakfast is served, is enclosed by six tall windows, transforming it into a semicircular solarium. Above each window a panel of red, purple, and blue stained glass adds festive splashes of color. Two lace-covered round tables seat eight, and because this spot is so delightful, guests are always reluctant to see breakfast end.

The second story is an open balustrade porch. Lattice work and two interior railings add an airy, garden-like mood to the interior. Guests may gaze through the living room, through the solarium and on to the secluded grassy yard and flower garden designed by John McClaren, the landscape architect of Golden Gate Park in San Francisco. The bright pink azaleas, the purple blossoms of the potato vine, and the orange bird of paradise create a vibrant range of color.

Cheryl is attentive to details, from providing fresh flowers to lighting the fireplace in the evening, lending romantic touches wherever possible. Each guest receives her personally prepared restaurant guide entitled "Our Favorites." Restaurants are categorized according to those "within walking distance," those "a short drive away" and those offering "ethnic fare." The ambiance, cuisine, and price range is detailed, making it a pleasure to find a place to dine. An all time favorite in the ethnic category, and not to be missed, is India Joze. Guests' selection of music by Mozart, Beethoven, Brahms, or Vivaldi begins at breakfast and plays through the day.

CLIFF CREST, 407 Cliff Street, Santa Cruz, CA 95060; (408) 427-2609; Cheryl McEnery, host. Five Rooms, each with private bath. Rates: $60 to $85. Includes breakfast of fresh fruits and breads, and boiled egg. No smoking; no children; no pets. Reservations occasionally made through answering service. Visa/MasterCard/American Express.

DIRECTIONS: from Rte. 17, which becomes Ocean Street, turn right onto San Lorenzo Blvd. Proceed 3 blocks and turn left onto Riverside Drive. Go over bridge, and turn right onto Third Street. At the top of the hill, turn left onto Cliff Street.

A ringside seat to all that Santa Cruz offers.

DARLING HOUSE

Seashore masterpiece

From sunrise to sunset the sight of surfers and yachts provides a spectacle from the front windows and porches of this seaside mansion. Bicyclers, skaters, walkers, joggers stream by too, intent on enjoying the three-and-a-half miles of unobstructed coastline that virtually begins at the Darling House.

Just as the flow of activity at the front door energizes, the gentle, warm feeling inside Darling House nurtures. These good vibrations emanate

from Karen, a nurse, and Darrell, a United Methodist pastor, poet, and social activist. Because they have always enjoyed a variety of people in their former professions, Karen and Darrell caringly and effortlessly share earnest conversation and genuine hospitality with guests.

The house is a William Week's Spanish revival, a masterpiece designed in 1910 for a Colorado cattle baron, complete with a triple arched veranda and a red tile roof. Seven kinds of wood including ebony, rosewood, and ribbon maple are elegantly and cleverly incorporated throughout. Sliding doors inlaid with delicately designed veneers match woods used on either side of adjacent rooms. Beveled glass windows and an art deco tile fireplace add to the remarkable craftsmanship of this home. And for those who enjoy puzzles, there is a prize for anyone finding the "flaw" in the fireplace!

DARLING HOUSE, 314 West Cliff Drive, Santa Cruz, CA 95060; (408) 458-1958; Karen and Darrell Darling, hosts. Seven rooms, all with sinks, share 2 ½ baths. Most rooms have an ocean view. Rates: $50 to $145. Includes a wonderful selection of fruits, homemade granola, and fancy breads for breakfast. Spanish and German spoken. Bicycles available. No smoking inside. No children or pets.

DIRECTIONS: from the north, Rte 1 becomes Mission Street. Turn right onto Bay Street and proceed to the ocean. Take a right onto West Cliff Drive.

NEW DAVENPORT BED & BREAKFAST INN

Spectacular coastline, special people

Just nine miles north of Santa Cruz, on Highway 1, the tiny community of Davenport resides along a magnificent stretch of California coastline. A good number of the two hundred populating the village are craftspeople (from a boat builder to a knife maker). Foremost among them are Marcia and Bruce McDougal.

After successfully operating the local Big Creek Pottery School, the McDougals opened the New Davenport Cash Store as an outlet for the school's pottery. It later evolved into a center for an outstanding selection of pottery, jewelry, textiles, and folk art from around the world. Shortly thereafter, they opened the New Davenport Restaurant, a casual establishment that offers wholesome, fine home cooking.

The New Davenport Bed and Breakfast is this energetic couple's newest addition to the community. Rooms are contemporary in design, and each is decorated with artwork and crafts. A wraparound porch on the second story of the main building is a wonderful place to relax and enjoy the beauty of the surrounding landscape.

A generous continental breakfast, which includes mouth-watering cinnamon rolls, is served in the small adjacent building, or guests may repair to the restaurant for a more full-bodied meal. Davenport is a great place to watch the gray whales as they migrate along the coast from January to May, or simply to pause from life's hectic pace.

NEW DAVENPORT BED & BREAKFAST INN, 31 Davenport Avenue, Davenport, CA 95017; (408) 425-1818 or 426-4122; Bruce and Marcia McDougal, owners. Twelve rooms; eight in two-story western-style building with a wrap around porch, four in adjacent restored home. All with private baths. Rates: $55 to $105. Includes a generous continental breakfast in sitting room. Exceptional cinnamon rolls! Complimentary champagne in each room. Children over twelve; no pets; smoking on the porches, sitting rooms, and dining room, but not in the bedrooms; Visa/MasterCard/American Express.

DIRECTIONS: on Rte. 1, halfway between San Francisco and Monterey Bay. Nine miles north of Santa Cruz. Slow down when you get to Davenport and you'll see it!

Hosts Marsha and Bruce McDougal. Overleaf, San Francisco seen from Marin County across the Golden Gate Bridge.

SAN FRANCISCO

THE MANSION HOTEL

Intentionally outlandish

The proprietor of the Mansion is Robert Pritikin, the same man who brought you *Christ Was An Adman*, America's most irreverent book on advertising. The place is a visual extravaganza, from the crimson pool table, surrounded by the Broadway set from Edward Albee's *Tiny Alice*, to the mural of pie-eating pigs at a picnic. The Mansion's macaw screeches in the background, while a human-sized Miss Piggy watches guests come and go from her chair on the stairway landing. Nightly performances by Pritikin on the saw, accompanied on the piano by Claudia, the resident ghost, and the weekend magic shows in the music room are examples of the zaniness to be encountered.

In addition to all the sophisticated gimmickry, The Mansion has one of the world's most extensive collections of Bufano sculpture and the building itself is quite splendid. Staying at the Mansion can be outrageous fun, and you will remember it vividly long after you've gone. Pritikin has put together a place that is intentionally outlandish.

THE MANSION HOTEL , 2220 Sacramento Street, San Francisco, CA 94115; (415) 929-9444; Robert C. Pritikin, Master of Ceremonies and owner; Denise Mitidieri, manager. Nineteen rooms, each with bath and special décor. Rates: $129 to $200. Includes expanded continental breakfast, plus a magic concert nightly. Pets allowed; all major credit cards.

DIRECTIONS: from Golden Gate Bridge, take Lombard Street for about one mile and turn right onto Divisadaro. Go one mile and turn left onto Sacramento and contiue for approximately two miles.

The Tom Thumb Room.

Miss Piggy enjoys guests' comings and goings.

The 1887 Mansion.

THE INN SAN FRANCISCO

The mood of Old World elegance

The mood at the Inn San Francisco is serene and harmonious. In the parlor, light through thickly fringed Victorian lampshades softly illuminates deep, dark green walls, heavy velvet draperies, and stained glass. Candles flicker on the marble mantel, and pretty porcelain adorns ornate tables.

The feeling of Old World elegance is carried to the bedrooms. There guests find old-fashioned lighting fixtures, Oriental rugs, brass beds—and perhaps a tub discreetly concealed behind a fabric screen or large dressing mirror.

Proprietor Joel Daily added dimension to his inn with an artful blend of contemporary conveniences. A second sitting room contains modular couches, a coffee table covered with books and magazines, a television, and a bulletin board that announces events around town. Slippered guests gravitate to this room to curl up with a book or relax in easy conversation. More luxury is available in the plant-filled solarium, where a hot tub beckons, and a spiral staircase leads to a redwood sundeck.

THE INN SAN FRANCISCO , 943 South Van Ness Avenue, San Francisco, CA 94110; (415) 641-0188; Joel Daily, owner; Miriam Wright, manager. Fifteen rooms, most with private baths, all with refrigerators, all with marble sinks and furnished in a Victorian tradition. Rates: $49 to $106. Includes hearty buffet breakfast with freshly squeezed orange juice, platter of cut tropical fruits, butter pastries, and hardcooked eggs. Children over 14; no pets; smoking allowed except in the parlor during breakfast; Visa/MasterCard/American Express. Limited parking by reservation.

DIRECTIONS: between 20th and 21st Street on south Van Ness.

Guests luxuriate in the hot tub, above, and socialize in the parlor, overleaf.

VICTORIAN INN ON THE PARK

Elegance in a superb location

Directly across from the verdant expanse of Golden Gate Park, the Victorian Inn on the Park was recently awarded landmark status. Innkeepers Lisa and William Benau's splendid Queen Anne-style inn was built in Queen Victoria's diamond jubilee year, 1897, and it supports one of the last remaining belvedere towers in the city. This grand, nine-thousand-square-foot mansion is filled with stunning architectural detail, from spectac-

ular fireplaces and broad staircases to elaborate wainscoting in spacious hallways. The fine inlaid wood floors and oak paneling in the dining room are good examples of the distinctive style of architect William Curlett and the impeccable taste of Congressman Clunie, who lived in the house for thirty years.

With advance notice, Lisa and Bill will present a chilled bottle of champagne to their newly arrived guests; they will make dinner reservations and confirm theater tickets as well. For the business traveler, the library is equipped with a large desk and telephone, and meetings or business luncheons are easily accommodated. Only ten minutes by car from downtown San Francisco, the Victorian Inn on the Park offers convenience as well as elegance.

VICTORIAN INN ON THE PARK, 301 Lyon Street, San Francisco, CA 94117; (415) 931-1830; Lisa and William Benau, hosts. Twelve rooms, each with private bath. Rates: $75 to $115. Includes continental breakfast of fresh fruits, freshly baked breads, and croissants. Children under ten discouraged; no pets; smoking is allowed with consideration to the preferences of other guests; Visa/MasterCard/American Express.

DIRECTIONS: from the airport, take US-101 and follow signs to Golden Gate Bridge. Exit at Fell Street and proceed on Fell approx 9/10ths of a mile to Lyon and the inn. From the south on US-101, exit at Lombard Street. Turn right onto Divisadero and proceed approx three miles. Take a right onto Fell and in three blocks a right onto Lyon.

Left and above, attention to detail distinguishes this lavish Victorian.

ARCHBISHOP'S MANSION

Where bed and breakfast achieves eminence

Quite simply, this is the most spectacular place to stay in San Francisco. Built for the archbishop of San Francisco in 1904, it survives today for the pleasure of its guests. The original three-story open staircase, with carved mahogany columns, soars upward to a sixteen-foot stained-glass dome. The expansive entry, hallways, and large rooms are characteristic of the Second French Empire style and suggest a grand country manor. Magnificently carved mantelpieces adorn eighteen fireplaces throughout the house, and high arched windows reflect the grandeur of its era.

Whatever has frayed with the passage of time has been restored with integrity. The resplendent painted ceiling in the parlor is fashioned after the decorative detail of a nineteenth-century Aubusson carpet. A stunning environment is created by the blending of Belle Epoque furnishings with Victorian and Louis XIV statuary, paintings, and bronze chandeliers.

Because Davis Symphony Hall and the opera house are nearby, limousine service for special evenings is provided. This kind of service is typical of the professional and accommodating style of proprietors Jonathan Shannon and Jeffrey Ross, who perfected the art of hospitality while presiding over the highly respected Spreckles Mansion. Anyone spending time at the Archbishop's Mansion is certain to feel pampered by the personal attention of a singular staff amid such resounding elegance.

THE ARCHBISHOP'S MANSION, 1000 Fulton Street, San Francisco, CA 94117; (415) 563-7872; Jonathan Shannon and Jeffrey Ross, owners. Fifteen rooms, all with private baths. Ten rooms have fireplaces, several are full suites with sitting rooms. Extraordinary décor. Rates: $98 to $300. Includes elaborate breakfast. Children discouraged; no pets; smoking is restricted to private rooms and Smoking Room; Visa/MasterCard/American Express. Off-street parking for eight cars and easy street parking. The public rooms are available to guests for cocktail parties and conferences; catering service.

DIRECTIONS: on northeast corner of Alamo Square at Steiner and Fulton. Alamo Square is six blocks west of the Civic Center and one block north of Fell.

Left, the opulence of the front parlor, and, above, the mansion seen from Alamo Square Park.

*Top left, La Boheme Suite and bottom
left, La Tosca Suite, both named after
operas, as are the other suites. Most can
accommodate business people.*

*Above, the second floor hallway shows
the grandeur of the mansion. Right,
owners Jonathan Shannon and Jeffrey
Ross, under the third-floor stained-glass
skylight.*

FAY MANSION INN

A majestic survivor of the earthquake

It is common belief that San Francisco's first operas were performed in the music room here by Maude Fay, a celebrated singer. Her family occupied this house from 1874 until 1957, and Maude counted Enrico Caruso as one of her many notable houseguests.

Understated elegance is the keynote here. One of the two tastefully appointed parlors serves as the music room, where a glistening black Kawai piano appears like a piece of sculpture. In the main parlor is one of the city's three hand-painted and stenciled ceiling frescoes still intact from pre-Earthquake days. Its delicacy is breathtaking, and its preservation is a blessing. Also surviving are the original brass and pot-metal chandeliers, with gaslight fixtures and globes beneath matching rosettes.

Standing majestically in the main parlor is a signed rosewood bibliothèque carved in the 1870s,

and an 1860s trumeau appears in its original unpainted state. In each of the bedrooms there are charming accents. A beaded handbag and knitted shawl lie across the foot of the bed in the Celebration Suite, and an antique lace dress hangs on the back of the door. Opera masks and elbow-length kid gloves adorn the Maude Fay Room, and there is plum wine with fortune cookies in the Madame Butterfly Room. Godiva chocolates tucked in a music box and a selection of French perfumes are just two of the touches indicative of the pleasantries here.

This intimate, romantic home can become a backdrop for a formal recital or a catered sit-down dinner, and both Sherris Goodwin, the owner, and Sandra Powell, the manager, are gracious and professional. The level of sophistication here is on a par with the best bed and breakfasts in San Francisco.

FAY MANSION INN, 834 Grove Street, San Francisco, CA 94117; (415) 921-1816; Sherris Goodwin, owner; Sandra Powell, general manager. Working knowledge of Spanish, German, and French. Five rooms, with two shared baths upstairs and ½ bath on main floor. Rates $69 to $150. Includes elaborate continental breakfast with a variety of cheeses, fruits, muffins, and unusual strudels and pastries. Confer with the manager regarding children under twelve; no pets; smoking permitted only on the porches and in the garden; personal checks accepted.

DIRECTIONS: on Grove Street, one block south of Alamo Square. Alamo Square is six blocks west of the Civic Center.

Left, original gas fixtures and painted ceiling in the exquisite parlor. Above, the Celebration Suite, enhanced by a marble fireplace, a mirrored 1870s walnut armoire, and a Louis XIV desk.

ALAMO SQUARE INN

A grand era revived

Wayne Corn, who was raised in North Carolina, and Klaus May, a native of Germany's Rhineland, make this the pleasant place it is. Innkeeper Wayne's brand of southern hospitality and resident-chef Klaus's European-style breakfasts herald the revival of that elegant era when continental-style accommodations and gracious service were commonplace.

Eliza Baum, a woman of vision, built this mansion. Inspired by the Midwinter Fair of 1894, with its far-reaching effects on building styles, the house is a blend of Queen Anne and Neo-Classical Revival. A grand staircase with hand-carved balusters, a stained-glass skylight, and large parlors hark back to an era when luxurious space was fashionable. Wainscoting, rich oak floors, and elegant furnishings blend with an eclectic collection of treasures from Afghanistan, India, Iran, and China.

A combination of Queen Anne and Neo-Classical Revival.

A contemporary look characterizes the furnishings of the morning room and adjacent solarium. Flower gardens have paths and decks to ensure a leisurely full breakfast or a relaxing time in the sun.

ALAMO SQUARE INN, 719 Scott Street, San Francisco, CA 94117; (415) 922-2055; Wayne Morris Corn, host; Klaus May, resident chef. Five rooms, each with private bath decorated in period pieces with oriental influence. Rates: $75 to $225. Includes hearty breakfast of eggs Benedict, omelets, breads. Special dinners and conferences by arrangement. Children over twelve; no pets; smoking in the solarium only; Visa/MasterCard/American Express.

DIRECTIONS: located on the west side of Alamo Square, ten blocks west of the Civic Center and two blocks north of Fell.

Sumptuous parlors blend Victorian and Oriental appointments.

INN ON CASTRO

Contemporary exuberance

In a town of traditionally furnished Victorian bed and breakfasts, the interior of this inn is very contemporary. Bedrooms, individually styled, are visually exciting—one includes a collection of hand-painted birds and another Oriental paper umbrellas.

Besides his penchant for interior design, innkeeper Joel Roman is also an artist. His bright, exuberant paintings of plant forms and glass objects hang throughout the house and underscore the playfulness of the decorating scheme.

Reflected on a chrome coffee table are dozens of pieces of blue glassware, while hundreds of brass, papier-mâché, stone, wood, and other ornaments cover the sideboard in the dining room. Lovingly collected are countless china place settings and interesting flatware. It is possible to spend a year here and never breakfast with the same tableware.

A radiant glass collection.

Joel is the quintessential innkeeper. If there is anything that can be provided for or arranged, consider it done. Whether you ask or not, you are likely to have nice things happen on your behalf.

INN ON CASTRO, 321 Castro Street, San Francisco, CA 94114; (415) 861-0321; Joel M. Roman, owner. French, Spanish, and fluent Italian. Five rooms with 2½ baths, shared. Rates $80 to $85. Includes full breakfast, of which half the fun is the table setting. Children "one at a time and well-behaved;" no pets; smoking permitted in bedrooms, but not in upstairs living or dining rooms; Visa/MasterCard/American Express. Bart subway and other public transportation at the doorstep. Restaurants within walking distance.

DIRECTIONS: located on Castro Street, just north of the intersection where Market, Castro, and 17th Streets meet.

The décor includes paintings by the host.

GOLD COUNTRY

THE HANFORD HOUSE

Wonderful hosts in the back country

Located in Sutter Creek, this two-story San Francisco style warehouse building, circa 1920, houses the Hanford House. Along with proprietors Jim and Lucille Jacobus, it boasts comfortable and well appointed furnishings, including Jim's grandfather's roll top desk in the front hall, Lucille's prized chest of drawers dating back to the days of Abraham Lincoln, and an expansive outdoor deck overlooking the countryside, hillside, and town.

Every fall, Sutter Creek plays host to an annual teddy bear and antique doll convention when people nationwide gather to show, buy, and sell. Poised and ready to greet them is the Jacobus' own collection of teddy bears that resides here in beds, on couches, on shelves, in closets: grandma bears, sailor bears, dancers, brides, grooms. "Hibernate at the Hanford House" says one little teddy bear's nightshirt.

Nearby there is lots to do: panning for gold, touring the wineries, browsing through antiques and specialty shops, exploring "gold rush" buildings and sites.

"If being successful in this business is based on friendliness, warmth, and caring, Lucille and Jim are number one. It's great to come home." This entry is scrawled in the Jacobus' breakfast room along with hundreds of other messages. The walls here are the guest book.

THE HANFORD HOUSE, Highway 49, 3 Hanford Street, P.O. Box 847, Sutter Creek, CA 95685; (209) 267-0747; Jim and Lucille Jacobus, hosts. Nine rooms, each with modern bath and ceiling fans. Rooms are newly constructed with high ceilings, are exceptionally large and beautifully appointed. Honeymoon suite has a fireplace. Rates: $55 to $100. Includes hearty breakfast of pastries, muffins, and platter of fruits & cheeses. No children under twelve; no pets; non-smokers rooms available; Visa/MasterCard. Facilities for handicapped include ramp and room custom-built to accommodate a wheelchair.

DIRECTIONS: located on Highway 49 near Main Street. The only two-story brick building in town!

Left, the sitting room. Above, the new inn building.

BOTTO COUNTRY INN

Across from the old Eureka mine

The Botto Country Inn sits directly across from what was the most productive vein of gold in the Mother Lode, the Eureka Mine. Hosts Stan and Mary Ann Stanton believe their two-story frame farmhouse gives visitors a true feeling for this historic area. From the broad and expansive porch, guests can see the stone granary that was once a thriving saloon. The age-worn structure conjures up visions of the miners who came to the saloon to celebrate a strike or to blot out their losses in a mighty oblivion.

There are sitting areas in all the guest rooms, variously named Violet Room, Oak Room, Four Poster Room, and Bird's Room. The Bird's Room features birds nests, bird prints, and other bird décor.

The inn is built on a hill overlooking the town of Sutter Creek, one of the prettiest and best-preserved villages in the entire gold country.

BOTTO COUNTRY INN, 11 Sutter Hill Road, Sutter Creek, CA 95685; (209) 267-5519; Stan and Mary Ann Stanton, owners. Five bedrooms with two shared baths. Rates: $63. Includes full breakfast of fresh fruit compôte, browned potatoes, scrambled eggs with herbs, sautéed vegetables, smoked ham in orange sauce or fritatas and sausage, french rolls, popovers, and champagne sherbert. No credit cards. Exceptional pets and well-behaved children welcomed. No smoking in bedrooms or bath-rooms.

DIRECTIONS: from north on Rte. 49 go through Sutter Creek up hill and turn left onto Sutter Hill Road. Proceed and you will see a stone building and Botto House on your right. From the south on Rte. 49 as you come down a hill before the town of Sutter Creek take a right onto Sutter Hill Road.

1871 stone granary adjacent to the 1914 farmhouse.

DUNBAR HOUSE

History and homey comfort

Dunbar House emanates romance, homey comfort, and history in equal measure. Innkeepers John and Barbara Carr are dedicated to the pursuit of serving their guests, and they succeed beautifully. A professional nurse for twenty years, Barbara provides a warm, relaxed atmosphere in which visitors can unwind. As she explains, "Guests come here to get away from it all, to enjoy the peace and quiet of the setting, and to regenerate the spirit. We constantly learn from them and love the variety of people who come to stay with us."

The town of Murphys is refreshingly simple. Main Street is filled with an attractive group of specialty shops, a museum, an old-fashioned ice cream parlor, and a small selection of restaurants. An abundance of well-preserved buildings evoke the days when Murphys was "Queen of the Sierras." Local lore has it that in just two weeks during the year 1860, miners took an unprece-dented $90,000 worth of gold from nearby mines.

DUNBAR HOUSE 1880, P.O. Box 1375, 271 Jones Street, Murphys, CA 95247; (209) 728-2897; John and Barbara Carr, hosts. Portugese spoken. Five rooms, two shared baths. Rates: $45 to $65. Mid-Winter, mid-week discounts. Includes buffet expanded continental breakfast with assorted cheese board, a variety of cereals and breads, and fresh fruit in season. Children over ten; no pets; smoking on the porches or in garden; no credit cards. Calaveras Big Tree State Park, wineries, skiing and Yosemite nearby.

DIRECTIONS: from Rte. 49 proceed to Angel's Camp. Go east on Rte. 4 for nine miles to the Business District turnoff. Take a left at the stop sign and the house is on the left at the Historical Monument.

Hostess Jane Grover likes to surprise guests with her period clothes.

OAK HILL RANCH

Keeping Victorian traditions alive

The opening scenes of *Little House on the Prairie* were shot within a mile of this yellow ranch house. No TV fictions here: the rolling hills, grazing cattle, and good clean air are a way of life in this part of the country.

The ranch reflects the tireless determination of its hosts, Sanford and Jane Grover, who twenty-five years ago began collecting Victorian turn posts, balconies, railings, mantelpieces, door-ways, and other turn-of-the-century relics that could be salvaged and incorporated into their recently built home. The result—a replica of a turn-of-the-century ranch house that is open, spacious, and airy.

The sophisticated country breakfast reflects Sanford and Jane's interest in gourmet food. Eggs Fantasia, baked with layered scallions, peppers, and fresh mushrooms, and Crêpe Normandy filled with chunky apple sauce and brandied raisins, are house specialties.

Devoted to Victorian traditions, Sanford remains active in the Horseless Carriage Club of America, of which he was president and board member for eleven years, and Jane, on occasion, loves to dress in period clothing. They always have at least one antique car. Both are active in community affairs, especially at the regional museum, which preserves the mining, logging, and railroad histories of the area.

Surrounded by fifty-six acres at the end of a long country lane, Oak Hill Ranch is everyone's ideal western farmhouse.

OAK HILL RANCH, 18550 Connally Lane, P.O. Box 307, Tuolumne, CA 95379; (209) 928-4717. Sanford and Jane Grover, hosts. Four bedrooms with two shared baths in main house, plus a private cottage with kitchen, living room, and fireplace ideal for honeymooners or families. Rates: $50 to $68. Includes a full country breakfast that is a delightful event. Children over fourteen; no pets; smoking on the outside porches and decks only; no credit cards. Close to Yosemite National Park.

DIRECTIONS: from Rte. 108, take Tuolumne Rd. to Carter St. Follow Carter St. south to the schoolyard and turn left onto Elm St. Take a right onto Apple Colony Rd. The sign for Oak Hill is on the left and will point you to Connally Lane. Proceed to the end of the lane.

A dramatic Victorian home, beautifully restored.

COMBELLACK-BLAIR HOUSE

A leap back in time

Walking into a bedroom at Combellack-Blair, one leaps back in time. It is as though the original owner of the house had just stepped away and left an assortment of combs, a hand mirror, and an enameled powder dish on her vanity. The pincushion is studded with needles and pins, and the embroidery, only partially finished, is set aside. Light glowing from the deeply fringed lampshade casts a soft pink shadow on the rocking chair, and the candles atop the washstand appear to be recently snuffed.

Oriental rugs and a collection of period furnishings in the front parlor recall the 1890s, when the prominent clothier, William Hill Combellack, built this home. Leading to the second floor and upward to the tower is an elegant spiral staircase.

Cecile and Jim Mazzuchi purchased the Combellack home after the family had lived there for seventy-nine years. Because the house is so beautiful and so much a part of Mother Lode history, the Mazzuchis decided to provide lodgings so that they could share it with others.

COMBELLACK-BLAIR HOUSE, 3059 Cedar Ravine, Placerville, CA 95667; (916) 622-3764; Cecile and Jim Mazzuchi, hosts. Two rooms with a shared bath. Victorian décor. Rates: $55. Includes a full breakfast with such things as home-made country sausage or sourdough pancakes, baked eggs, homemade English muffins, and in the afternoons, various cakes and three kinds of freshly baked cookies. No children; no pets; smoking allowed on outside balcony or porches; no credit cards. Snoopy is the dog in residence. Placerville is in the foothills of the Sierra Nevada mountains with many historic sites nearby.

DIRECTIONS: from Sacramento on Rte. 50, exit onto Bedford and then make a right onto Main St. At the monument, take a right onto Cedar Ravine and the house is on the left.

MURPHY'S INN

A third-generation innkeeper

"A good innkeeper provides his guests with as many comforts as possible, whether it's keeping a fire blazing on the hearth or helping to plan a day of sightseeing."

A heritage of innkeeping that spans seventy-five years has imbued Marc and Rose Murphy with a true understanding of the nature of the business. Murphy's Inn was built in 1866 as an estate for a famous gold baron. One of the loveliest homes in town, it is also among the most pleasant inns in all the Mother Lode country. The living room is filled with lovely antiques, and the lace curtains and floral wallpapers in the bedrooms gently evoke the past.

From the big and sunny breakfast room, guests watch Marc, in the open kitchen, as he concocts a delicious morning repast that might include Belgian waffles or coddled eggs. Each bedroom has a call button, which will bring Marc or Rose to the door bearing a breakfast tray.

A sports enthusiast, Marc loves to share his knowledge of the area. Visitors enjoy excellent cross-country and downhill skiing, swimming, jogging, and golf privileges at the nearby Auburn Country Club.

MURPHY'S INN, 318 Neal Street, Grass Valley, CA 95945; (916) 273-6873; Marc and Rose Murphy, hosts. Eight rooms, six with private bath. Rates: $48 to $88. Includes full breakfast with such delights as coddled eggs or Belgian waffles. Mid-week discounts, business rates, ski packages. Well-behaved children; nearby kennel facilities for pets; smoking permitted in designated areas; major credit cards. Parakeets, Jerry the cat, and Pearl the Staffordshire bull terrier in residence.

DIRECTIONS: from the south, take Rte. 49 north to Grass Valley and exit at 174/Central Grass Valley. Turn left at the first stop sign onto south Auburn and then left at second stoplight which is Neal Street. Continue three blocks to the corner of Neal and School Street.

The gracious interior suggests a genteel lifestyle.

GOLDEN ORE HOUSE

A gourmet spree

This is the place to have the best homemade scones and Scottish oat cakes in all the Gold Country. Breakfasts are a gourmet spree, with a special egg entrée and innkeeper Donna Rail's own blend of fresh-roasted Sierra Mountain coffee. Afternoon tea boasts delicious homemade tea cakes—Scotland's finest—and herb or nut cream cheese spread.

The turn-of-the-century house was renovated and restored by owner and builder Wayne Peterson, whose ingenuity is ever present. A marvelous, railed deck off the second-floor sitting room beckons guests to catch a bit of sun or read beside an umbrella-covered table. The skylights and built-in bureaus in the upstairs bedrooms and bathrooms are made with natural materials that blend well with the original redwood wainscoting, fir floors, and antiques.

GOLDEN ORE HOUSE, 448 South Auburn Street, Grass Valley, CA 95949; (916) 272-6872; Donna Rail, host. Six rooms, three with private baths. Three downstairs rooms are Victorian, three upstairs are contemporary with skylights and built-in furniture. Rates: $50 to $75. Includes sumptuous full breakfast and afternoon tea. Children by arrangement; no pets; no smoking; Visa/MasterCard.

DIRECTIONS: from Sacramento on I-80, take Rte. 49 north. Follow 24 miles to Empire Street exit and turn right. Proceed several blocks and turn left onto South Auburn. Continue 3 blocks; the inn is on the left.

No-nonsense lions guard the entrance.

THE VICTORIAN

A museum of antiques, silver, and crystal

After a career in retail clothing and a stint as the first woman president of Auburn's chamber of commerce, Maurine Cook is now raising funds to restore Auburn's capitol building. Having traveled the world over, she has ensconced herself atop a hill in a 134-year-old house centered on seven acres overlooking the town of Auburn. With interests as far reaching as the 4-H club and the D.A.R., Maurine is as tenacious as they come, and there is little she is not up to handling with authority and style.

The Victorian, one of the oldest homes in the area, is a museum of antiques, silver, and crystal collected over a lifetime. It has a formal living room and an elegant dining room. For relaxing, the pool, the hot tub, and the well-tended gardens are especially inviting.

Maurine is protective of her privacy, so it is especially important to call ahead. Once she expects you, however, she will show you how much she loves to provide a home for travelers and obviously succeeds. "Hardly a guest leaves here without throwing their arms around me and giving me a big hug," she grins.

THE VICTORIAN, P.O. Box 9097, Auburn, CA 95604; (916) 88: 5879; Maurine Cook, owner. Three rooms share 1 full bath a 2 half baths. Rates: $45 to $65. Includes full breakfast of waffl (made from grandma's recipes), fruits, bacon or ham. Childr over twelve; no pets; smoking is permitted, but not in t bedrooms; no credit cards. Pool, hot tub and garden, patio a gazebo.

DIRECTIONS: call for directions; the home is open by appoir ment only.

Owner Annette Meade.

The impressive white colonial revival home presides at the "Top of Broad Street," a block above the heart of one of California's most delightful and historical gold mining communities. A fanciful three story residence, it has open verandas in front and enclosed back porches overlooking the gardens on the first and second stories, which seem to recall the wealth and style of bygone gold fortunes.

At breakfast, guests select their own duck motif mug from dozens hanging in the huge pine breakfront in the dining room. Such little touches, Annette hopes, help make guests feel at home. Next to a dish of jellybeans, on the coffee table in the living room, antique children's blocks spell out WELCOME.

GRANDMERE'S, 449 Broad Street, P.O. Box 1628, Nevada City, CA 95959; (916) 265-4660; Annette Meade, host. Six attractive country style rooms, each with private, artistically tiled bath. Several rooms can accommodate three or four guests, one room has a kitchen and separate entrance. Rates: $75 to $115. Includes gourmet French country breakfast. Covered parking. Indoor spa. Television and VCR in sitting room. Manicured grounds. No smoking; no pets; Visa/MasterCard.

DIRECTIONS: from I-80, take Highway 49 for 27 miles. Take offramp at Broad Street and turn left onto Broad. Proceed through town 3 to 4 blocks; the house is on the left.

GRANDMERE'S

Where grown-ups are spoiled

Although this house appears formal, Annette Meade creates a casual and amiable mood at Grandmere's. She is an amazing woman who, besides being a weaver and quilt maker, is an inspired woodworker who made most of the Shaker-style chests, cradles, and cabinets throughout the house.

The interior of the house is painted pale grey and crisp white and stylishly carpeted in a cool grey. This monochromatic palette provides a quiet backdrop for the blaze of colorful quilts, of the bold folk art of Charles Wysocki, and wicker baskets of bright flowers. There are two means of ascent and descent here: a grand staircase in the front hallway and a state-of-the-art antique elevator.

Handmade quilts on all the beds.

WINE COUNTRY

Furnished with the finest American antiques.

OVERVIEW FARM

A real treasure

A sense of comfort prevails at Overview Farm. Tall madrones, manicured gardens, cordoned fruit trees, and thoughtfully placed garden benches offering wide vistas or cozy seclusion provide the perfect, park-like setting.

Tucked into the foothills, the white 1880's farmhouse has spacious country grandeur. Part of the famed Spreckels summer estate, this single-story house, on the National Register of Historic Places, is architecturally simple. The tall windows, glass enclosed porch entry, twelve foot high ceilings, skylighted hallway, and generously large rooms, make Overview quite remarkable.

The early American antiques that hosts Judy and Robert Weiss have collected are worth noting—a large spinning wheel made of maple and oak has its origin in the Northeast in the 1840's; a dining room corner cupboard with bullet molding dates back to 1790. A pair of early folk art paintings of a boy and girl flank the fireplace, heavy brass candlesticks decorate the mantel, and a reproducing grand piano works perfectly.

The furnishings are inherently simple, but in this spacious home they exude elegance. Plush carpeting, fine quilts, and carefully selected furniture enhance each of the guest rooms. Fluted crystal, pewter service, and fine silver and linens embellish the breakfast table.

After touring the wineries it is a lovely place to come back to. A rose garden and captivating view complement the beauty of the interior.

OVERVIEW FARM, 15650 Arnold Drive, Sonoma, CA 95476; (707) 938-8574; Judy and Robert Weiss, hosts. Three large rooms, tastefully decorated, each with private bath. Two have fireplaces and the third is a two-room suite. Rates: $85. Includes lavish full breakfast served with eggs as you like them and sausage or bacon in addition to fruits and breads. No children; no pets; no smoking; no credit cards. Sasparilla is the Cairn Terrier in residence.

DIRECTIONS: proceed through the town of Sonoma and go north on Rte. 12 for 5 miles and take a left onto Madronne. Follow to end and take a left onto Arnold. Go about 300 yards to white rail fence and turn right at the sign. Proceed straight to top of the hill.

Owners Judy and Robert Weiss.

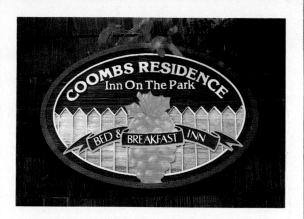

COOMBES RESIDENCE

A balance between past and present

Built in 1852, this brown-shingled home trimmed in white, stands proudly on the edge of Fuller Park in downtown Napa and is one of the oldest surviving residences.

Rena Ruby, refreshingly spunky and forthright, maintains a pleasant balance between the cherished things of the past and those of the present. A formal parlor charms with its floral wallpaper, mahogany trim, antique upright piano, and a one-hundred-year-old oak round top display case filled with an arrangement of dried flowers. In contrast, there is an invitingly comfortable living room, complete with the latest magazines and a color TV. Other rooms have Oriental carpets, wrought iron beds, and claw foot tubs, while outside there is a large pool and Jacuzzi.

Exquisite hand-pressed linens and white duvets, elaborately finished with fine needlework and fluffed to perfection accent the bedrooms. Lace trimmed white pillows, some woven with pastel satin ribbons, complete the delicate effect.

COOMBES RESIDENCE, 720 Seminary, Napa, CA 94559; (707) 257-0789; Rena Ruby, host. Four rooms, sharing 2½ baths. Rates: $70 to $85. Includes continental breakfast with house blend of coffee and afternoon refreshments. Swimming pool and Jacuzzi. Bicycles available. No children; no pets; smoking only in common rooms; Visa/MasterCard.

DIRECTIONS: Rte. 29 to First Street exit. Proceed to 2nd Street and take a left. After 5 or 6 lights take a right onto Seminary.

LA RÉSIDENCE

For lovers of haute cuisine

Gothic Revival built by a New Orleans river pilot.

"I have such wonderful memories of sitting in English country inns with a room full of strangers and everyone trading stories over a glass of wine," mused hostess Barbara Littenberg, "so I thought it would be fun to open my own." Apparently the fun has not faded. Her favorite part of the business is still welcoming guests and sharing experiences over a glass of wine.

Innkeeping suits her so well, in fact, that she has doubled the initial size of La Résidence to include what is affectionately referred to as "the Barn"—a structure decorated in a French country style, with double French doors that open out onto decks and patios. The Main House, an 1870s Gothic Revival, has a distinct southern flavor accented by interesting period antiques.

There are four top restaurants within twenty minutes of the inn: Auberge Soleil, Miramonte, Domain Chandon, and the French Laundry. Haute cuisine is so popular in the area that Barbara plans to conduct cooking seminars with guest chefs in the Barn's professional kitchens. Special wine courses, wine tastings, and tours are offered here.

LA RÉSIDENCE , 4066 St. Helena Highway N., Napa, CA 94558; (707) 253-0337; Barbara Littenberg, hostess. Fifteen rooms total, most with private baths, some with fireplaces; 7 are in the main house, "The Victorian;" 8 are in the "Barn," with balconies and patios. Rates: $65 to $115. Includes expanded continental breakfast and wine. Children over fourteen; no pets; Visa/ MasterCard/American Express.

DIRECTIONS: from San Francisco, US-101 to Rte. 37 to Rte. 12. Proceed onto Rte. 29 to North Napa and turn right after Salvador Ave.

A spacious and alluring bedroom adds to the romance of a weekend of wine tasting.

The beautiful Blue Room has a seven-foot carved headboard, and a working Victrola.

GALLERY OSGOOD

Napa Valley's most lavish breakfast

For innkeepers and artists Joan Osgood and Howard Moehrke, the "good life" means delicious food, interesting conversation, the comforts of a lovely home, and art. Joan's special creations include delicate silkscreen prints, on view throughout the house, and a lavish breakfast that ranks among the best in the Napa Valley. Howard, also an expert in computer software, is responsible for the stained-glass that glows from many windows. These colorful, contemporary works of art provide a charming counterpoint to this Queen Anne–style, redwood home, built in 1898. The three guest bedrooms are in keeping with the age of the house—a hand-crank Victrola adds an old-fashioned flavor to the Blue Room, the Rose Room is filled with wicker and lace, and the Poppy Room features a queen-size iron bed and poppies everywhere. Joan sees to it that guest rooms are scented with fresh flowers, and bouquets often include fragrant blossoms from the inn's camellia trees.

Joan and Howard are enthusiastic guides to the area and can summarize the individual attributes of each of the neighboring wineries.

GALLERY OSGOOD, 2230 First Street, Napa, CA 94559; (707) 224-0100; Joan Osgood & Howard Moehrke, hosts. Three rooms, one shared bath. Rates $77 double. Includes lavish, gourmet breakfast of plentiful proportions and guests are invited to join the hosts for a glass of wine. Children over fourteen; no pets; Visa/MasterCard. Pet dog, Heidi is a Llasa Apso and outdoor cat Hershey is part Persian.

DIRECTIONS: from the south on Rte. 29 exit at First Street/Central Napa. Proceed on exit ramp and take a left onto Second St. In one block take a left onto Seymour St. and then a left onto First St. The inn is on the right.

Owners Janet and Geoffrey Villiers

OLD WORLD INN

Homemade truffles

Running this eight-room inn is like being on permanent holiday for Janet and Geoffrey Villiers, compared to their strenuous days spent managing the full-service hotel they had in England. These British innkeepers have a refreshing sense of humor and delight in being host and hostess. Their collective energy goes directly into providing the niceties, a goodly portion of which is the generous assortment of food.

Beginning at breakfast, there are muffins, croissants, sweet rolls, and poppy seed cakes. A main entrée of crêpes or pancakes is beautifully accompanied by an arrangement of decoratively sliced fruits.

Tea time is an event as only the English can make it. Scottish shortbread, date pinwheels, and chocolate cake are but a few of the homemade treats. At wine tasting hour around 5:30 or 6 P.M., eight gourmet cheeses are presented with French bread, crackers, fresh vegetables, and a savory dip.

But it is at dessert time that Janet and Geoffrey really excel. Quipped Janet, "After an evening out, didn't we always come home and raid the fridge?" Bite-size macaroons, green mints, and amaretto torte too good to believe, chocolate box cake made of crushed cookies, pistachios, and grand marnier, and assorted truffles all provide that "little something" to satisfy a late night snack urge.

OLD WORLD INN, 1301 Jefferson Street, Napa, CA 94559; (707) 257-0112; Janet and Geoffrey Villiers, hosts. Eight rooms, each with private bath. Rates: $75 to $100 weekends; $55 to $80 weekdays. Includes an abundance of foods from morning to just before midnight! Custom built Jacuzzi. No children; no pets; no smoking in the house; Visa/MasterCard/American Express.

DIRECTIONS: from San Francisco via Golden Gate Bridge: north on Rte. 101 to exit 37; follow to Rte. 121 and then left onto Rte. 29. Take Lincoln East exit, proceed ½ mile, and make a right onto Jefferson.

The Carl Larsson Room is the consummate bridal suite.

VILLA ST. HELENA

Rooms with vineyard views

The scale of the Villa is impressive at thirteen thousand square feet, and yet the symmetry and simplicity of its architecture encourages informality. The wood paneled library is cozy and comforting should one want to quietly peruse the extensive collection of wine related books and magazines. In contrast, the living room is very grand and festive with warmth generated by sun pouring in from the solarium or from a fire burning in the huge stone hearth.

Hundreds of cymbidium orchids florish in the courtyard, solarium and on the verandas under the watchful eye of owners Ralph and Carol Cotton. Sharing their villa is a joy, as there is a particular elegance to the palatial home and splendid grounds. The expansive grassy courtyard lures guests to step out from glass enclosed verandas and enjoy lounging by or swimming in the Villa's spacious pool. The backdrop for the pool and its adjacent patio and brick barbeque is an eliptical arched red brick wall carved into the hillside, creating a harmonious blend of natural beauty and masterful design. So fabulous is the setting that this courtyard was chosen for the shooting of a few party scenes for "Falcon-crest."

VILLA ST. HELENA, 2727 Sulphur Springs Avenue, St. Helena, CA 94574; (707) 963-2514; Ralph & Carol Cotton, owners. Three suites, each with private bath and spacious quarters. Rates: $145 to $185. Special mid-week rates. Includes a bountiful and delicious breakfast served in solarium, with a selection of cheeses and bread and a variety of baked or fresh fruits. Complimentary bottle of wine each evening. No children; no pets; Visa/MasterCard/American Express. Nutmeg is the cat in residence.

DIRECTIONS: from Rte. 29 take a left onto Sulphur Springs Ave. Proceed approximately 1½ miles and look for sign on mail boxes on the left. Take a left and follow the private driveway ¾ of a mile to the top of the hill.

AMBROSE BIERCE HOUSE

The former home of a literary legend

Set back off the main artery to all the Napa Valley vineyards, this house was home to writer Ambrose Bierce, who mysteriously disappeared in 1913, on a trip to war-torn Mexico. Recalling Bierce's days here the suites have been named after figures who touched the writer's life: Lillie Langtry, star of the Edwardian stage; Eadweard Muybridge, father of the motion picture, and Lillie Coit, the legendary belle of San Francisco and Bierce's good friend.

Carefully renovated, this charming post-Victorian house has comfortable furnishings and a nicely appointed period look. There are lots of fresh flowers in season and always a profusion of house plants. Proprietors Tony Prince, formerly a USA to Britain tour operator, and his travel-savvy wife, Sheila, have been operating this bed and breakfast to perfection. The Princes reside on the lower floor, and the upper part of the house, complete with its own parlor, is the domain of their guests. Guests mingle easily in this atmosphere and a house party quickly develops.

Berringer's, one of the Napa Valley's premier wineries, is within walking distance of the bed and breakfast, as are four of the valley's finest French restaurants—Rose et Le Favour, Miramonte, La Belle Helène, and Le Rhône.

THE AMBROSE BIERCE HOUSE, 1515 Main Street, St. Helena, CA 94574; (707) 963-3003; Tony and Sheila Prince, owners. Two rooms, one suite, all with private baths. Designer coordinated décor. Rates: $75 to $135. Includes continental breakfast with fruit course and different types of croissant. Children twelve and over; no pets; smoking in common areas only, not in the bedrooms; American Express.

DIRECTIONS: fifteen miles north of Napa on Rte. 29, which becomes Main St. On the north end of St. Helena, two doors off Pine St. on the west side of the street.

Memorabilia, from period cameras to vintage firearms, add historical character to the Eadweard Muybridge Room.

There are graceful porches on four sides of the perfectly symmetrical house.

THE INK HOUSE

An architectural achievement

This Victorian farmhouse is an architectural achievement in perfect symmetry. Each side is identical and each looks out on a vineyard. Built a century ago, this intriguing home reflects the character and ingenuity of Theron H. Ink, a man of many interests.

Twelve-foot-high ceilings make the rooms feel large and spacious. The bedrooms have American and English oak and walnut furniture, lace curtains, and handmade quilts. An informal but inviting parlor is furnished with a plum velvet settee and matching side chairs, Victorian marble tables, and an Oriental carpet. Breakfast is served on a large oak table in the crystal-chandeliered dining room. Bran muffins, raisin-carrot or banana-nut cakes, and fresh fruit are offered.

The Clarks moved into the Ink House with their five children in 1967. Ten years later they started their inn. The children still stop by to help with the chores, answer the phone, make reservations, and take over the innkeeping when mom and dad take time off. This is a family-run business that makes other families feel right at home. A glass of sherry from one of the local wineries awaits you.

THE INK HOUSE, 1575 St. Helena Highway, St. Helena, CA 94574; (707) 963-3890; Lois Clark, hostess. Four rooms, each with private bathroom and shower. Furnished with antiques. Rates: $70 to $90. Includes breakfast of juice, nutbread, cereals, muffins, tea, coffee. No children under twelve; no pets; no smoking; no credit cards. Three dogs and one cat in residence but not in guest areas.

DIRECTIONS: at the southwest corner of Rte. 29 and Whitehall Lane, three miles south of St. Helena.

CALISTOGA COUNTRY LODGE

Where East meets West

Described by some as the place where the sensibilities of Georgia O'Keefe, Mat Dillon, and Pocahontas meet, this lodge is definitely "out west." Antlers, steer skulls, cowhides, and relics of the Western frontier are ever-present and a trophy caribou, with a double shovel rack, presides over the stone hearth. Brightly colored Navaho rugs provide the color accents to the all-white decor of the expansive Common Room, along with a rose colored abstract painting by Ira Yeager. Large canvas umbrellas add flair to the natural logpole pine furniture covered with canvas or cowhides designed by the Lodge's owner Tom Scheibal. Wide, whitewashed floorboards, large windows, and potted trees enhance the crisp and open mood.

Breakfast is served buffet style and is refreshingly casual and relaxed. Gourmet coffee is poured from a big campfire coffee pot, and scones are warmed in a small white porcelain oven which appears to be right off the chuck wagon. Guests help themselves and either return to their rooms, settle down in the Common Room, or take their breakfasts outside to relax by the pool. Others nibble a bit, take a swim and then linger in the sun while finishing off fruits, and almond pastries.

Tucked into several acres of orchards with lovely views of the mountains, guests are tempted to lounge in the courtyard between adventures into Calistoga and neighboring wineries.

Guests find it easy to relax and socialize by the pool and in the Common Room.

CALISTOGA COUNTRY LODGE, 2883 Foothill Blvd. Calistoga, CA 94515; (707) 942-5555; Becca Smith, host; Tom Scheibal, owner. Six rooms, three with private baths, remaining three share one bath. Rates: $75 to $85. Includes lovely continental buffet breakfast. No children; no pets. Visa/MasterCard & American Express. Large pool with surrounding courtyard.

DIRECTIONS: take Rte. 29 to Calistoga and proceed straight through stoplight; the Inn is ½ mile north on the left.

Owners Jan and Scott Sofie.

BRANNON COTTAGE INN

Inspired simplicity

In *Silverado Squatters*, Robert Louis Stevenson wrote of Sam Brannon's Calistoga Hot Springs Resort in 1880: ". . . lawns run about the house, surrounded by a system of little cottages, each with a veranda and weedy palm before the door . . . and a very pleasant way this is, by which you have a little cottage of your own, without domestic burdens by the day or by the week."

With an abundance of creativity and enthusi-

asm, Jan and Scott Sofie used their ingenuity to refurbish the last surviving guest cottage on its original site. Jan, owner of a natural fiber clothing store, and Scott, a respected chef, combined their talents on this attractive restoration.

Five arches of the front porch, painted a crisp white with forest green detailing, create a charming entry to this 1862 Greek Revival cottage. The lovely gardens and quiet courtyard continue to delight visitors more than a century later.

The intentional sweet simplicity of Brannan Cottage befits its origin as a sanctuary for travelers seeking rejuvenation. The soft rose parlor walls and the deeper rose velvet furnishings harmonize well, and the subdued colors of each guest room complement the original hand-painted stencils which Jan designed to depict local flowers: wild Iris, California poppies, morning glories.

BRANNAN COTTAGE INN, 109 Wapoo Avenue, Calistoga, CA 94515; (707) 942-4200; Jan and Scott Sofie, hosts. Six rooms, all with private baths and private entrances. Rates $85 to $95 weekends; $75 to $85 mid-week. Includes full breakfast. Bit of French, Spanish, and German spoken. Children are welcome by arrangement, especially as the young charmer of the family, Andrew Sofic, enjoys company. Pets are considered if they promise to get along with Lily, the Bearded Collie and Cosmo, the handsome Gorden. Smoking allowed in rooms but not in parlors. Visa/MasterCard. Handicap Access.

DIRECTIONS: north on Rte. 29 to Calistoga. Right on Lincoln Avenue (main street) past Glider Airport. Left onto Wapoo.

Left, the gigantic, sun-filled bedrooms contain some of their original furnishings.

MADRONA MANOR

A gourmet's bed and breakfast

Built as a vacation retreat for a wealthy San Francisco businessman in 1881, expense appears to have been of no concern here. The ceilings are high, and the several parlors off the hallway are large and elegant. A broad staircase leads to four spacious master suites, each of which either has a large bay window or opens out onto a balcony.

Many of the furnishings in both the Manor and adjacent Carriage House are original to the estate and are important examples of American Victorian Renaissance style. There is an elegant mahogany four-poster bed dating from the mid-1800s and a full suite of matching carved walnut and burled wood dressers and headboard. The music room of the Manor remains the same, with the original rosewood square grand piano still in place.

Part of the eight-acre estate is planted with luxurious flower gardens and a citrus grove.

Foxgloves, delphineums, tulips, iris, daffodils, sweet peas, and zinnias find their way into the rooms. "People from the east who have never picked an orange go out and do it and think it's just wonderful," laughs owner Carol Muir.

What was at one time the billiard room is now one of the two dining rooms of Madrona Manor, where gourmet meals are served to guests and to the public. The cuisine is orchestrated by several chefs who use a brick oven, smokehouse, orchard and vegetable-herb garden to provide memorable meals. Having a restaurant in-house adds an unexpected luxury to this grand bed and breakfast estate.

MADRONA MANOR, 1001 Westside Road, Box 818, Healdsburg, CA 95448; (707) 433-4231; Carol and John Muir, owners; Todd Muir, resident chef, Denice Fitzgerald, pastry chef. John Fitzgerald, resident landscape architect, and Mark Muir, resident maintenance manager (all family). Twenty rooms, some with fireplaces, all with private baths; nine in manor and balance in carriage house and adjacent buildings. Rates: $80 to $125. Includes full breakfast in dining room or on outdoor terrace. Children welcome; manageable pets by arrangement; smoking allowed but guests are requested not to smoke in bed; Visa/MasterCard/American Express. Wheelchair access to one downstairs bedroom. Swimming pool.

DIRECTIONS: from US-101, take the second Healdsburg exit. At the first stoplight, make a left onto Mill Street. In approximately ¾ of a mile the road turns to the left and the arched white gateway to the manor is straight ahead.

CAMELLIA INN

Simple grace and elegance

Built in 1869, the Camellia Inn is an early example of an Italianate Victorian building whose lines are exceptionally simple and graceful. Keeping the Victorian furnishings to a refreshing minimum allows the architecture to speak for itself. High ceilings, twin white marble fireplaces in two adjacent parlors, and tall, arched windows are all enhanced by natural light reflected off the salmon colored walls. Silk-screened wallpaper, a hand-crocheted bedspread, and satin pillows add just the right touches in the guest rooms.

Two of the rooms, Moon Glow and Demitasse, are in the main house and share a classic 1920s green-tiled bathroom. Moon Glow is named for the soft moonlight that shines through the cedar trees into the spacious room. Demitasse, overlooking an outdoor fishpond, is named for its coziness and charm. The remaining four rooms, located in a separate building, are reached by

The quiet elegance of the entrance hall, above, and the classic proportions of the building, right, give the 1869 home a sophisticated urban look.

crossing a small patio. A favorite room, once the original dining room of the home, and now called the Royalty Suite, has a massive maple tester bed brought from a castle in Scotland.

Camellia Inn is a wonderful place to visit in any season. On chilly mornings a fire in the breakfast room adds romance as well as warmth. In summer, you can sip a glass of wine under the shade trees near the large swimming pool.

A stay at the Camellia Inn often includes a tour of owners' Ray and Del Lewand's home-style winemaking facilities.

CAMELLIA INN, 211 North Street, Healdsburg, CA 95448; (707) 433-8182; Ray and Del Lewand, owners. Seven rooms, five with private baths. Several with private entrances. Each furnished with period antiques. Rates: $45 to $70. Includes full breakfast of fresh fruit, homemade breads, and eggs. Guests are invited to join the hosts for wine and cheese in the evening. Children by special arrangement during the week; no pets; smoking in the parlors, but not in bedrooms; Visa/MasterCard. Swimming pool. Two blocks from town square. Over 40 wineries within seven miles and good fishing for steelhead not far away.

DIRECTIONS: from US-101 take the second Healdsburg exit. Proceed north for three blocks and turn right onto North Street.

Angles, eaves, and arches define the upstairs rooms.

GRAPE LEAF INN

Chardonnay Suite, Pinot Noir Room

In what appears to be a small house of no particular architectural note, the playfulness of the Grape Leaf Inn comes as a surprise. It is hard to believe that there are seven bedrooms tucked into this house. The first floor is unadorned and cozy, with several overstuffed couches and a dining table snugly fitted into one room. But upstairs the Grape Leaf comes alive. The second floor has been totally remodeled, and four of the bedrooms have been built under the attic eaves.

Each of the upstairs rooms has two to four dormer windows to let in an abundance of light. The dramatic roof, dormers, and arches are accented with mirrors, stained-glass, and decorative wood, making the space whimsical and vibrant. Each room, named after a different grape, is decorated to match the grape's color. There is a rose-accented Gamay Room, a yellow and white Chardonnay Suite, and a Pinot Noir Room trimmed in purple.

Best of all is the attention given to the bathrooms. All four upstairs rooms have modern tiled baths, with large skylights over spacious whirlpool tub/showers for two.

GRAPE LEAF INN, 539 Johnson Street, Healdsburg, CA 95448; (707) 433-8140; Terry Sweet, owner. Kathy Cookson, hostess. Seven rooms, each with private bath. Three are traditional period rooms and four are remodeled to combine contemporary styles. Four upstairs rooms have whirlpool tubs/showers for two. Rates: $55 to $95. Includes full breakfast with homemade breads and egg dish. No children under twelve; no pets; smoking outside only; Visa/MasterCard. Downstairs rooms are wheelchair accessible.

DIRECTIONS: take second Healdsburg exit and proceed on Healdsburg Av. Take a right onto Grant St. and the Grape Leaf is two blocks on the right at the corner of Johnson and Grant.

FOOTHILL HOUSE

Upbeat hospitality

Michael and Susan Clow, Foothill's youthful and exhuberant innkeepers, are absolutely committed to pleasing their visitors. "We do everything we can to make our guests glad they are here with us," notes Susan. "Our bedtime turn down service is a nice surprise—we light the fireplaces, fluff pillows, put in fresh towels, and set out a decanter of sherry and a plate of warm cookies."

The color scheme for each of the four suites is based on the fabrics chosen for the elaborate quilts Susan has sewn. Every detail in décor and convenience has been considered to enhance the suites. Four poster beds, comfortable chairs or sofas by the fireplace, refrigerators for chilling wine and cassette players provide everything a person could desire.

FOOTHILL HOUSE, 3037 Foothill Blvd. Calistoga, CA 94515; (707) 942-6933; Michael and Susan Clow, hosts. Four suites with private baths, fireplaces, refrigerators, air conditioning, and ceiling fans. Each with separate entrance and patio. Rates $65 to $95. Includes continental breakfast with beautifully presented fruit and a variety of breads. Guests join their hosts for wine tastings in the evenings. Well-behaved children over 12; no pets; smoking on patios or outside porches only; Visa/MasterCard. Several cats in residence.

DIRECTIONS: take Rte. 29 North to Calistoga. At the blinking light where Lincoln Ave. intersects 29, proceed straight. Highway 29 becomes Foothill Blvd. Go 1½ miles; Foothill House is on the left.

The Evergreen Suite, with private patio.

TOLL HOUSE INN

A fascinating hostess

Originally spoken by the young men of this valley from 1880 to 1920, Boontling is the jargon you'll hear in this little town. Basically a vocabulary of one thousand words, the language provided menfolk with a private tongue, which, as evidenced by some of the puzzling signs you'll see, is enjoying a renaissance. "Horn of zeese for the applehead" means ordering a cup of coffee for your girl.

A visitor does not have to speak Boontling to feel at home at Bev Nesbitt's Toll House Inn. Because Bev is so adept at anticipating needs, her guests need little in the way of vocabulary except plenty of thank-yous. She is gracious and kind, with the virtues of an aunt with the knack for helping relatives relax and enjoy themselves. Her interesting and varied background, which includes everything from cattle ranching, trucking, and commercial fishing to modeling and surfing makes her a fascinating woman.

Fabulous breakfasts are served up in a sunny dining room, and gourmet dinners are available by reservation. The rooms are large, inviting, and furnished in stylish good taste. There is a wonderful patio, hot tub, and attractive perennial garden.

TOLL HOUSE INN, P.O. Box 268, 15301 Highway 253, Boonville, CA 95415; (707) 895-3630; Beverly Nesbitt, hostess. Five rooms, two suites with private baths and fireplaces. Rates: $60 to $95. Includes a full breakfast with fresh fruits, omelets, biscuits or muffins. Complimentary wine in each room. Children over twelve; no pets; no credit cards. Raley the dog and Aimee the cat in residence. Located in a secluded valley in the heart of Mendocino wine country.

DIRECTIONS: from San Francisco take US-101 North to Rte. 253 west, and proceed for 11 miles to the inn. From Boonville junction of Rte. 128 and Rte. 253 turn east for 6 miles to inn.

HOPE-BOSWORTH HOPE-MERRILL

Two restored homes reflect different periods

Careful research and painstaking attention to detail by innkeepers Bob and Rosalie Hope are evident throughout their Hope-Merrill and Hope-Bosworth homes. The houses, across from each other on Geyserville's main street, reflect different periods and therefore differing styles and moods.

Hope-Merrill, built around the 1880s, is an Eastlake and Stick Victorian with formal lines. The interior is similar in design, with elegant wainscoting, a carved banister on a curved stairway, and high graceful windows. The home has been awarded accolades for its authentic décor, which includes lovely period antiques, a Victorian dollhouse, a fire screen embroidered with calla lilies, Parrish lithographs, and bountiful displays of Victorian memorabilia, including a glass case of beaded handbags.

Hope-Bosworth, built in 1904, is a "pattern-book house," built from plans selected and ordered from catalogues offering the popular contemporary styles of the day. It is predictably simpler in design and mood. The building is more square, and the rooms are symmetrical; the staircase climbs at utilitarian right angles. With pale oak and wicker furnishings and patterned wallpapers, the overall décor is less ceremonious, giving a country feeling to the house. Tall palm trees, more than seventy feet high, stand at the entrance to Hope-Bosworth, and a white picket fence encloses the yard.

The houses provide an interesting and educational glimpse into bygone eras that suited two particular life-styles. Today, either provides a lovely base from which to explore the wineries and recreational activities of the Russian River and surrounding countryside.

HOPE-BOSWORTH and HOPE-MERRILL, 21238 Geyserville Ave., Geyserville, CA 95441; (707) 857-3356; Bob & Rosalie Hope, owners. Five rooms in one house, seven the other. Private, half, and shared baths. Rates: $50 to $75. Includes a continental breakfast with fruits and breads. No children; no pets; smoking only in designated areas and not in bedrooms; Visa/MasterCard/American Express. Outdoor Jacuzzi and pool. Special wine tours conducted from the premises. Catered dinners by advance reservation.

DIRECTIONS: from US-101, exit at Geyserville; the houses are across the street from one another on the main street of Geyserville.

Elegantly restored guest rooms: in the Hope-Merrill, left, and the Hope-Bosworth, above.

NORTHERN CALIFORNIA

THE PELICAN INN

Shakespeare could have slept here

Perfectly natural in its wooded seaside setting, this sixteenth-century-style English country manor exudes the hospitality and comfort of the old English pub and inn. A fire blazes on the full hearth, and folks are gathered with mugs of ale or cups of mulled wine cheering players at the dart board. Meat pies and Scotch eggs are served on long, candlelit wooden tables. And as the English might say, there is good fellowship in plentiful proportions.

Upstairs are six rooms, all continuing the sixteenth-century theme. Canopied beds, lovely antiques, and recessed leaded windows enhance the feeling of taking a step back in time. There is even a step stool to help you get into the high old bed.

Never has a 400-year-old inn, restaurant, and pub been so authentically replicated. It is the realization of one man's dream, Charles Felix, who wanted to resurrect a family hotel in Surrey that went back five generations. Built in 1977, and twenty minutes from San Francisco, the Pelican is indeed in another world. The fascination and appeal of the Pelican are perhaps best reflected by the need to reserve a weekend six months in advance.

THE PELICAN INN, Muir Beach, CA 94965; (415) 383-6000; Charles and Brenda Felix, publicans; Kathy Burford, reservations manager. Six rooms, each with private bath and shower. Queen-size beds and half testers in each very English room. Rates: $95. Includes a hearty English breakfast of eggs, bangers (English pork sausages), fruit, and broiled tomatoes. Children are allowed and rollaway beds are available; pets allowed; Visa/MasterCard. A cat, Sheba, a Dachshund named Banger, and a great Dane named Dekan are in residence.

DIRECTIONS: twenty minutes from Golden Gate Bridge on Rte. 1. From US-101, take Stinson Beach/Highway 1 exit and stay to the left.

Left, the coastline from the porch of Whale Watch Inn (page 106). Above, the Pelican Inn.

BLACKTHORNE INN

A magical place

The Blackthorne is a product of the late sixties and early seventies, when people were building adventurous, nonconformist dream houses. Located in a canyon near Point Reyes National Seashore, it is a stunning example of an imaginative person's nontraditional approaches to living space. The Blackthorne, in fact, looks like an elegant treehouse.

Endlessly fascinating with its multiple levels, the Blackthorne is a series of interconnecting decks, handcrafted details, stained-glass windows, skylights—and a firepole for the limber to get from one level to another. There is a large stone hearth, laid by the Blackthorne's owner.

A four-story spiral staircase leads to an octagonal room in the building's tower. Known as the Eagle's Nest, the room has windows on every side and can also be reached by a forty-foot catwalk that connects with the highest of four decks. A thick blue carpet and Japanese futon are the only furnishings, making the treetops and sky the true decorative elements.

Perfect for the young at heart, the Blackthorne is one of the most romantic of the bed and breakfasts. There is every convenience here, including modern shared bathrooms, full hearty breakfasts, and the opportunity to try side-by-side tubs on a redwood deck. The Blackthorne is magical.

BLACKTHORNE INN, P.O. Box 712, Inverness, CA 94937; (415) 663-8621; Bill Wigert, owner; Susan and Bill Hemphill, managers. Five rooms with shared baths. Rates: $85 to $125. Includes expanded continental breakfast of fruits, cereals, yogurt, breads, quiche, and coffee cakes. No children; no pets; Visa/MasterCard. Pt. Reyes National Seashore nearby with miles of hiking trails and beautiful seashore.

DIRECTIONS: take US-101 to Sir Francis Drake Blvd. exit and proceed west to Olema. Take a right turn onto Rte. 1. Proceed about two miles and make a left turn towards Inverness. Go 1 mile and take a left onto Vallejo just before Perry's Inverness Park Grocery.

Left above, the Eagle's Nest, the most romantic, magical room on the coast.

ELK COVE INN

For a romantic weekend by the sea

Perched strategically on a bluff overlooking the powerful Pacific and one of its sheltered coves, Elk Cove Inn is the perfect destination for a romantic weekend by the sea. The main house is a Victorian cottage that contains several bedrooms, a dining room, a living room with working fireplace, and a library. A short distance away, attached by a walkway, a separate redwood structure houses several comfortable bedrooms with beamed ceilings. Just past the inn's old-fashioned flower garden, a staircase to the beach beckons.

Innkeeper Hildrun-Uta Triebess has welcomed guests into her home for two decades. A spirited hostess, she is well known for her talent in the kitchen. Breakfast is full and generous and often includes German egg cakes or omelets. For the convenience and delight of her guests, as well as the occasional outsider, Hildrun-Uta serves a multicourse continental dinner, included in the price of the stay. Guests might enjoy coq au vin blanc, salmon in sour cream, or poached meatballs in lemon-caper sauce.

ELK COVE INN , Highway One, P.O. Box 367, Elk, CA 95432; (707) 877-3321; Hildrun-Uta Triebess, hostess. German, French, Spanish, Italian spoken. Four rooms with private baths in two cabins, two with skylights and fireplaces. Five rooms in nearby guesthouse with shared baths. All rooms have spectacular ocean views. Rates: $98 to $148 weekends; $62 to $98 weekdays. Includes a full breakfast of German egg cakes or omelets and a German or French dinner of several courses. Children over twelve; no pets; smoking on decks and porches; Visa/MasterCard. Baasco is a friendly pygmy goat in residence.

DIRECTIONS: located on Rte. 1, 15 miles south of Mendocino. From US-101 north exit at Cloverdale and take Rte. 128 west to the coast and go five miles south on Rte. 1.

A stone's throw from a dramatic beach—see overleaf.

The elaborate bed was used in the movie Wuthering Heights.

THE OLD MILANO HOTEL

Spectacular views of the ocean

Built in 1905 near cliff-hanging railroad tracks, this old hotel offers spectacular views. Though no longer part of the scene, the railroad is remembered. The owners have bought a caboose, placed it in their woods, and furnished it to perfection for the railfan. Formerly used by the North Pacific Coast Railroad, it has a guest suite for two, with kitchenette and observation cupola.

The hotel's six grand guest rooms overlook the ocean, and are furnished with antique armoires and curious beds, including an oak sleigh bed. Pale green floral William Morris wallpaper distinguishes the lavish, plushly furnished formal parlor. Stones collected from local beaches were used to make a large fireplace in an adjacent parlor, where wine from the hotel's extensive collection of Northern California wines is served in the evenings.

An additional option for guests is the white clapboard Passion Vine Cottage, located on the hotel grounds. Covered in salmon-colored passion flowers, it is fitted with a sleeping loft, sitting room, and small kitchen.

THE OLD MILANO HOTEL, 38300 Highway 1, Gualala, CA 95445; (707) 884-3256; Leslie Linsheid and Collette Tessier, owners. Nine rooms, including a Caboose, a cottage, and remarkable suite with a private sitting room overlooking the ocean. Private and shared baths. Open all year. Rates: $75 to $150. Includes continental breakfast. No children; no pets; no smoking in the house. Visa/MasterCard/American Express. Hot tub. Massages available by certified practitioner. Excellent dining in restaurant on premises, featuring fresh foods daily.

DIRECTIONS: on Rte. 1 one mile north of Gualala; the entrance to the hotel is on the left.

A unique guest room.

WHALE WATCH INN

Gray whale vantage point

At the Whale Watch Inn, natural beauty and refreshing salt sea breezes vanquish the stress and tension of everyday life. The inn is a complex of contemporary buildings designed so that every room commands a sweeping view of the southern Mendocino coastline. Besides the vistas, the flicker of firelight in each guest's chamber creates a romantic atmosphere in the cool of the evening. If guests desire to remain in a private world of their own, breakfast is delivered to the door each morning. Those in a more gregarious mood gather for their morning meal in front of a circular fireplace in the hexagonal Whale Watch Room. A light and sustaining fare of fruits, breads, yogurt, and cheeses starts the day off right.

The weather pattern along this patch of coast is atypical. Known as "the banana belt," the Gualala area is free from the thick fogs that frequently blanket much of the northern coast of California. The result is an unparalleled vantage point on the pathway of the migrating gray whales that travel along the coast from winter to spring.

WHALE WATCH INN BY THE SEA, 35100 Highway 1, Gualala, CA 95445; (707) 884-3667; Irene & Enoch Stewart, owners; Beth Bergen, hostess. Eighteen rooms in five contemporary buildings, each with private bath, several with full kitchens and fireplaces, all with private decks, suites, and spas. Rates: $105 to $185. Includes continental breakfast of fresh fruits, fresh breads, cheese or yogurt. No children; no pets; no smoking; Visa/MasterCard/American Express. Stairs to private sheltered beach.

DIRECTIONS: from San Francisco take US-101 to Petaluma and proceed west through Two Rock and Valley Ford to Bodega Bay. Follow Hwy 1 north to Whale Watch at Anchor Bay, 5 miles north of Gualala.

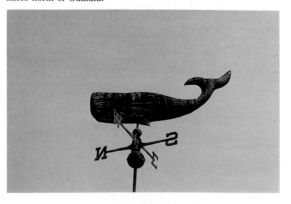

Right, Howard Creek Ranch, an oceanside retreat

HOWARD CREEK RANCH

Rural retreat by the sea

Bordered by the vast Pacific Ocean and set in a secluded valley surrounded by lush green farm country, Howard Creek Ranch is perfect for those who cannot decide whether to vacation in the country or stop by the sea. The main complex here comprises two back-to-back New England-style farmhouses furnished in true country fashion, with a fireplace, overstuffed furniture, and the unexpected—like a moose head over the piano. One of the guest rooms has a private balcony. With a loft bed under a skylight, the other guest room looks out on the stars.

For those who like to rough it, there's the hull of a fishing boat that has somehow grown into a cabin complete with a galley kitchen, patchwork-quilt-covered bed, and a large picture window overlooking the creek. For those even more adventurous, another rustic cabin provides cold running water and a wood-burning stove.

Howard Creek Ranch provides the opportunity for beachcombing, swimming in a fresh-water creek, and bike riding along the beach—all offered up with country-style hospitality.

Many of the guests enjoy horseback riding along the beach or up through the hills while others relax on the lawn and keep an eye out for the blue heron and other species of birds.

Sally's flower garden fills the air with a sweet scent. The vibrant colors of her garden, the rolling countryside, and the sandy beaches combine to make this a very sensational place for travelers who want to experience a full complement of what California has to offer.

HOWARD CREEK RANCH, P.O. Box 121, Westport CA 95488; (707) 964-6725; Charles and Sally Lasselle-Griggs, owners. German, Dutch, French, Italian spoken. Three rooms in main house with two shared baths, plus a cabin converted from a boat, a cabin with skylights and an ocean view, and a rustic cabin. Rates: $45 to $75. Includes a hearty ranch breakfast of hotcakes, eggs, bacon or sausage. Children and pets often welcome by previous arrangement; no credit cards. Swimming pool filled with fresh creek water. Hot tub and sauna heated by wood. Massage by reservation.

DIRECTIONS: located on Rte. 1, three miles north of Westport. Entrance is by milepost 80.49. Turn east and bear left and you'll see big white farmhouse.

1021 MAIN STREET

Thrilling panoramic vista

As the only inn in the town of Mendocino on the oceanside of Main, 1021 Main Street offers the most exceptional, unobstructed vista available. The floor-to-ceiling windows in the dining room, the natural wood sundeck trimmed with plants and driftwood, and manicured lawn making a path through tall beach grass down to the ocean, render the scene idyllic.

1021 Main is quintessential Mendocino, as it was originally conceived—a haven for the individualist. Marilyn, having lived here for almost twenty years, is a vital and creative artist whose talents range from theater to interior design. Stepping into her home, which reflects her eclectic taste, is both a priviledge and adventure. Her penchant for the avant garde is present in the fur covered couches and a Jungian-inspired, jowl-like woodstove she commissioned a local sculptor to build for her. Adorned with serpentine chimney pipes, it is affectionately called Hot Lips. Her passion for the rustic is seen in the knotted rope banister, and her attraction to the traditional is displayed by the sophisticated Belgian tapestries, Persian carpets, and 200-year-old painted Oriental rice paper screens.

The sun deck of the main house.

The two Cottages, are equally diverse in flavor and ambiance. The Foundry is a tin roofed A-frame, with windows opening onto a secluded little garden patio. It has a sleeping loft accessible by ladder and a circular sunken shower-tub. Couches, wood stove, refrigerator and a dining table make this a writer's hideaway. The Zen House, perched in the beach grass, has to be one of the most seductive, inspirational spots in the world. White kapis shell screens open to a sensational view of the Mendocino Headlands. Low Oriental furnishings, bamboo-lined shower, and cast-iron stove on a platform of small stones create a mood attested to in a poem penned by former guests, "We entered your door, little Zen House, and were filled with enchantment and awe. For all that we saw, we felt we needed . . . "

The Zen House in the foreground perches right above the ocean.

Left, The Foundry, the perfect winter retreat.

1021 MAIN STREET GUEST HOUSE, 1021 Main Street, Mendocino, CA 95460; (707) 937-5150; Marilyn Solomon, host. Two rooms in main house, each with sink, share one bath. Two extraordinary cottages. Rates: $75 to $115. Includes breakfast of fresh fruits and delectable homemade goodies such as crustless quiche or fancy crêpes. No children under 16; no pets; smoking in cottages and common areas, but not in bedrooms of main house; no credit cards.

DIRECTIONS: from Rte. 1, turn west towards the center of town and follow to Main Street.

Left, Victoriana and exquisite craftsmanship combine to create a striking redwood exterior. Above, Christi and Mark Carter share a sense of history as they stand in front of their spectacular house.

THE CARTER HOUSE

Re-creation of an earthquake casualty

Mark Carter found his dream house in a book of Victorian architecture at a friend's antiques store. The original house in San Francisco, destroyed in the earthquake of 1906, had been designed in 1884 by Samuel and Joseph Newson, who were also the architects of Eureka's famous Carson Mansion. Using the Newson's plans, Mark, with the help of several young assistants, re-created the house a century later. It took him sixteen months to complete his masterpiece of modern-day craftsmanship.

Extraordinarily fine antiques grace the parlors and dining room, but unlike Victorian homes, it has no dark or somber interior. White walls and marble floors blend with natural polished oak and redwood wainscoting, making all of the rooms bright and open. Contemporary paintings and graphics by local artists hang throughout the house. These, along with porcelain and ceramic pieces, are for sale in the Carters' first-floor art gallery. Woven baskets filled with potted mums are everywhere.

Breakfasts are prepared by Christi Carter, who formerly owned a restaurant and ice cream parlor. Pear, Grand Marnier, and almond phyllo tarts are not beyond her delectable repertoire.

Hospitality comes easily to the Carters, who serve cocktails and hors d'oeuvres in the evening, and cordials, tea, and cookies as a late-night snack. They are delighted to tell you about nearby Old Town, which is an impressive restoration of the surrounding waterfront, and to share with you their enthusiasm for the splendors of Eureka, of which they are so prominently a part.

THE CARTER HOUSE, Third & L Streets, Eureka, CA 95501; (707) 445-1390; Mark and Christi Carter, hosts. Seven rooms, private and shared baths. Wheelchair access to ground floor rooms. Rates $50 to $175. Includes an elegant, full breakfast of fresh fruit, an egg dish, muffins, and delicate pastries. Cordials in the afternoon, tea or coffee and homemade treats in the evening. Business rates mid-week: $35 to $65, single with continental breakfast. No children or pets; smoking on main floor, but not in rooms; Visa/MasterCard.

DIRECTIONS: take 101 into North Eureka and go west on L Street.

This Carpenter Gothic house is filled with antiques and treasures collected over a lifetime.

SHAW HOUSE INN

A superb example of Carpenter Gothic

The bed in Shaw House Inn's Honeymoon Suite is the same bed used by local couples a hundred years ago who were married by Seth Shaw, Justice of the Peace and founder of Ferndale. Seth Lewis Shaw's home, begun in 1854 and completed in 1866, has endured as a remarkable contribution to the historical integrity of the area. The elaborate Victorian Gothic Revival house of steep gables, recessed porches, intricate gingerbread trim, and balconies is set along the creek that Shaw first navigated into this valley. Built on land he cleared of overgrown ferns, the house is a tribute to his pioneering spirit and signaled the beginning of farming in this community.

The house was always open to visitors and travelers in Shaw's time, and innkeeper Velna Polizzi (formerly an antiques dealer) shares this tradition. Her dedication to the preservation of this house and her high regard for the historical renaissance in Ferndale are everywhere evident in her restoration of the home to its previous splendor. The formal parlor, dining room, and bedrooms echo the refinements of an earlier era. She has added, as well, her lifelong collection of fine glass, art, china, and other antiques, including some of museum quality.

SHAW HOUSE INN, 703 Main Street, Ferndale, CA 95536; (707) 786-9958; Velna Polizzi, owner. Five rooms, private and shared baths. Rates: $45 to $75. Includes full breakfast of fresh fruit compote, egg dish, bread. Children sufficiently responsible to take their own rooms are welcome; no pets; smoking on outside balconies and porches only; no credit cards. Lady Amber Ashley is cat in residence.

DIRECTIONS: from US-101, exit at Ferndale. Proceed about 5 miles and the sign for Shaw House is on the right.

Left, the garden-like bathroom, decorated with imported French floral wallpaper. The inn, above, is a gingerbread classic.

GINGERBREAD MANSION

Everything adds to the fantasy

Years ago, when the town wanted to tear it down, two gentlemen bought this house. They spent eighteen years restoring it, and one of them, a landscape gardener, created the beautiful and unusual topiary, something rarely seen in this country.

A spectacular peach and yellow high-Victorian, the Gingerbread Mansion has delicate woodwork around turrets, gables, tower, and porches. Two camellia bushes, shaped into trees, stand guard in front of the house and add to the fantasy. Called the "Butterfat Palaces of Cream City," houses like this one were built for Ferndale's successful dairy farmers.

Wendy Hatfield and Ken Torbert bought the mansion four years ago and turned it into a bed and breakfast. The furnishings are eclectic. Pieces include Victorian settees, Eastlake tables, and carved French armoires, as well as a variety of patterned wallpapers, a bird's-eye maple fireplace, Oriental carpets, and wood-burning Franklin stoves.

Each day, one of a variety of delicious breads— lemon, pumpkin, or cranberry-apple—is served for breakfast, and Wendy's bran muffins are becoming famous.

Little extras add personal warmth to the elegance. Turned-down beds, bathrobes, early-morning coffee or tea, vintage bicycles for exploring back roads into canyons, and boots and umbrellas if it rains are amenities appreciated by guests who stop here.

THE GINGERBREAD MANSION, 400 Berding Street, Ferndale, CA 95536; (707) 786-4000; Wendy Hatfield and Ken Torbert, hosts. Fluent in Spanish and Portuguese with some French and Japanese. Eight rooms, five with private baths, three share. Two claw-footed tubs, toe-to-toe in one guest room. Rates: $55 to $85. Includes a generous continental breakfast of fresh fruit platter, selection of fruit breads and local cheeses. Afternoon tea with cake and sweets at bedtime. Children ten and over welcome; no pets; no smoking permitted in the house, but there is a veranda off the second floor with chairs, lap blanket, and ashtrays to accommodate smokers; Visa/MasterCard.

DIRECTIONS: from US-101, exit at Ferndale. Proceed about five miles into town and turn left onto Brown Street at the Bank of America. The house is ahead on the left one block.

THE PLOUGH AND THE STARS COUNTRY INN

Hosts Melissa and Bill Hans.

A lighthearted, casual atmosphere

When Melissa and Bill Hans discovered a century-old farmhouse in the far reaches of Humboldt County, they visualized a dream come true. Combining Bill's love for the country with Melissa's professional background in food and restaurant management, they created a charming rural inn whose warm hospitality typifies bed and breakfast travel. The inn is especially snug and congenial on cool and misty days when guests can warm themselves by the fire blazing in the hearth. And for sunny days there is a spacious patio.

After a breakfast of Melissa's fresh-baked breads and succulent fruit topped with a generous dollop of *crème fraîche*, visitors may enjoy a game of croquet on the lawn or a drive into Arcata. There are shops, restaurants, and a movie theater, where for two dollars you can catch a double feature of classic films.

THE PLOUGH AND THE STARS COUNTRY INN, 1800 27th Street, Arcata, CA 95521; (707) 822-8236; Bill and Melissa Hans, hosts. Five rooms with shared baths. Upstairs sitting room. Rates: $35 to $57. Winter rates discounted. Includes a full continental breakfast of strawberries and *crème frêche* in season and English muffins or toast and sweet bread. Eggs and bacon prepared for slight additional charge. Children over twelve; outdoor pets by arrangement, but will need to get along with friendly black Labrador, Hannah, and three cats; no credit cards. Wheelchair access to ground-floor room.

DIRECTIONS: on US-101 north, exit at Somoa Blvd. Loop up over freeway heading West for about ½ a mile. Take a right onto K St. Continue on K St., which bends to the left and becomes Alliance Rd., and take a left onto 27th St. The sign and the inn are ³⁄₁₀ of a mile on the right.

Built in the 1860s in the flatlands of scenic Humboldt County.

The view of the cove from the inn is fascinating because the weather is constantly changing.

TRINIDAD BED BREAKFAST

Beachcombers' delight

The view of the harbor is unforgettable from this Cape Cod home 175 feet above the quiet cove of Trinidad Bay. A sleepy village of about 400 people, Trinidad has a winter fishing fleet of seventeen boats that anchor here. In summertime the number increases to over 300 boats and yachts bobbing in the cove. They are protected from the ocean swells, often twenty and thirty feet high, by a jetty of land known as Trinidad Head.

While exploring nearby trails around Trinidad Head, walkers end up at the most westerly point of land in California, where whales and otters are easily spotted. On one side the ocean crashes against the rocky coastline, on the other side lies a calm, protected bay. A favorite excursion along an old stagecoach road leads down to Indian Beach where beachcombers delight in the driftwood that washes ashore. The two major redwood national parks, a thirty minute drive in either direction, makes this location ideal for outdoor buffs.

Innkeepers Carol and Paul Kirk couldn't be more hospitable. Having raised a family and toiled in the corporate world, they settled quite happily into this rural community. Early in the morning Paul might be glimpsed in his overalls en route to oversee their family run restaurant. Carol might already be kneading dough for the morning meal. Rockers by the brick fireplace on an enclosed porch and attractively decorated guest rooms with magnificent views make this a particularly wonderful place to be. Whether the fog is rolling in or the sun is shining, the ever changing scene enhanced by the distant clang of buoy bells is magical.

TRINIDAD BED & BREAKFAST, Edwards Street, P.O. Box 569. Trinidad, CA 85570; (707) 677-0840; Carol and Paul Kirk, hosts. Three rooms, two share one adjoining bath and third has private bath and separate entrance. Rates: $65 to $85. Winter Rates available. Includes continental breakfast of fruits and warm breads. Extraordinary view of Trinidad Bay with trails to beach and lighthouse. No pets; no small children; smoking on balcony or porch; no credit cards.

DIRECTIONS: from the south on Rte. 101, exit at Trinidad and follow Main Street through town. With the bay straight ahead, the inn is on the left.

OREGON

CLIFF HARBOR HOUSE

Where nature restores your spirit

There is no coastline in North America that compares with Oregon's expansive beaches, roaring surf, and buffeting winds. Here nature's power is revealed in the most elemental way. You can feel its forces reenergizing you.

Respite from the elements is offered by Cliff Harbor Guest House, overlooking the spectacular rocks and surf of Bandon beach in southern Oregon. You can watch the foaming breakers, the cormorants, the puffins from a cushioned window seat while Luciano Pavarotti's voice swells in the background from the living room stereo.

Cliff Harbor's unbelievably beautiful setting constantly renews the spirit. Doris and Bill Duncan knew that when they built their private retreat. Guests are welcomed and can stay in two comfortably modern redwood suites. The largest has a freestanding fireplace, a full kitchen, a dressing table, two double beds, and a view of the west, where most evenings one can see the glorious colors of the setting sun sinking into the Pacific Ocean. The hospitality of the Duncans allows fortunate guests to experience the exhilarating, wild beauty of the Oregon coast from a safe haven.

The old section of Bandon, formerly the main part of town, is experiencing a renaissance and is now chock-a-block with restaurants, artisans, craft shops, jewelers, and a nationally recognized art gallery.

CLIFF HARBOR GUEST HOUSE, P.O. Box 769, Bandon, OR 97411; (503) 347-3956, 344-4132; Doris and Bill Dunean, hosts. Two spacious, modern suites, both with private entrances and private baths. One has wheelchair access, the other has fireplace and kitchen. Rates: $52 to $65 double. Slightly less during the winter. Includes a wonderful full breakfast with rolls or cranberry bread, fluffy omelets or eggs, and bacon. Children welcome; no pets; no credit cards.

DIRECTIONS: provided upon reservation confirmation.

Left, sea grass covers the dunes behind the inn, which overlooks the scenic wonder of Bandon beach, above. OVERLEAF: *view of the inn, the beach, and the colorful gorse, or Irish furze, brought from Bandon, Ireland, by the town's founder, Lord Bennet.*

ROMEO INN

Poolside pleasantries

Tea time at Romeo Inn gives host and hostess Bruce and Margaret Halverson an opportunity to welcome their guests graciously. Hot hors d'oeuvres, cheese cookies, or pastry, along with great grandmother's china tea cups make this a pleasant tradition. In the cooler months, tea is served in the living room of this charming Cape Cod home. In warmer weather, guests gravitate to the beautifully secluded patio and pool. Breakfast may be served outside at poolside tables on request. Lounge chairs, a Jacuzzi, a brick barbecue grill, and a hammock strung between a couple of shady trees are so comforting that it is sometimes difficult to pry oneself away to enjoy the various theatrical performances for which Ashland is noted.

The inn, located in a residential section of Ashland, sits on the side of a hill amidst big pine trees and within walking distance of the Shakespearian Theater and downtown shops and restaurants.

ROMEO INN, 295 Idaho Street, Ashland OR 97520; (503) 488-0884; Bruce and Margaret Halverson, hosts. Four rooms, each with private bath. Two are very large with private entrances; one with fireplace. Rates: $75 to $100. Includes full breakfast of egg dish or waffles, ham or bacon and afternoon tea. Landscaped patio with pool and spa. Central air-conditioning. No children; no pets; no smoking; no credit cards. Handicap access.

DIRECTIONS: from Siskiyou Blvd, turn west onto Sherman Street. In two blocks turn right onto Iowa, and in one block turn left onto Idaho. The inn is one block ahead on the right.

CHANTICLEER BED & BREAKFAST INN

Salmon quiche or cheese blintzes?

An exterior view of Jim and Nancy Beaver's Chanticleer Bed and Breakfast Inn reveals a simple and well-proportioned Craftsman bungalow whose strength of character derives from the softly hued porch constructed of native river stone. Entering the inn, one is captivated by its country-French interior.

The six guest bedrooms are a refreshing and sprightly mix of pastel wall coverings, coordinated floral sheets and puffy down comforters, fresh flowers, and rich carpeting. In the first-floor living room, Nancy's lustrous Haviland china collection is displayed in a glass case.

Each morning Jim and Nancy serve an especially generous and delicious breakfast in the dining room, whose windows open onto the foothills of the Cascade Mountains.

Ashland is justly famous for its high-quality Shakespeare festival, which runs year-round. Each season, the festival stages four to six Shakespeare plays as well as American classics and one original play.

CHANTICLEER BED & BREAKFAST INN, 120 Gresham Street, Ashland, OR 97520; (503) 482-1919; Jim and Nancy Beaver, hosts. Six rooms and one suite, each with private bath. Decorated in a fresh French country style. Rates: $69 to $79; suite $99. Includes full breakfast with fruit course, and main entrée of baked eggs, salmon quiche, or cheese blinzes, coffee cake or croissant. Children welcome by prior arrangement; no pets; no smoking in bedrooms; no credit cards.

DIRECTIONS: from the south on I-5 take Siskiyou Av. exit and turn left on Third St. (just after sign for public library). Proceed ½ block on 3rd which becomes Gresham. From the north on I-5 take the first Ashland exit to Rte. 99 and turn left; 99 becomes Main St. Turn right onto Gresham just before Public Library.

portico. A landscaped circular drive brings guests to the house, where the Siskiyou and Cascade Mountain Ranges hover in the background. There are sweeping views of the mountains from inside the house, especially from the carpeted sunporch where Phyllis's homemade pastries entice guests to linger over breakfast.

The mountains can also be enjoyed from each of the bedrooms, which are pleasantly filled with antiques, homemade quilts, and thoughtful little extras. Guests are welcome throughout the day to relax with coffee or tea in the book-filled parlor.

MORICAL HOUSE, 668 North Main Street, Ashland, OR 97520; (503) 482-2254; Joe and Phyllis Morical, hosts. Five rooms, each with private bath. Rates: $65. Off-season rates are less. Includes breakfast of fruits with yogurt topping, breads, and baked egg dish with vegetables and cheese, and an afternoon snack. Air-conditioned. Children are welcome by arrangement; no pets; smoking permitted execpt in dining room. Located on Ashland's busy main thoroughfare, a 15–20 minute walk from downtown.

DIRECTIONS: from the north on I-5 take the first Ashland Exit and follow signs toward town. After the "City Limit" sign, Morical is the first house on the left. From the south, proceed straight through town to where two-way traffic begins; the inn is 9/10 mile on the right.

MORICAL HOUSE

A masterpiece of landscaping

"Absolutely everyone has to putt," exclaims hostess Phyllis Morical, when talking about her husband's most engaging landscaping endeavor— a putting green. In addition to the variety of putters available at the house, there are pitching wedges for those who need to practice their approach shots.

Joe Morical, who took a master gardener course, has elaborately landscaped over 10,000 square feet of the lawn surrounding the house with over 100 varieties of colorfully fragrant trees, shrubs, and flowers. Guests often relax on the lawn among the flowers to read or sunbathe before sightseeing and theater-going.

Turning off the highway onto Morical grounds, one glimpses the welcoming 1880's bungalow-style Victorian with its large inviting covered

Left, the McCully Room, which contains a portrait of Jane McCully, the original owner.

McCULLY HOUSE INN

1861 historic landmark

Jacksonville was a booming tent town basking in the glory of the Gold Rush when town physician and real estate speculator John McCully decided to build a palatial home befitting a gentleman of his stature. Soon after it was finished, however, his debts got the best of him, and he stole out of town in the dead of the night never to be heard from again. His wife Jane, being resourceful, turned the twelve room home into a boarding house, furnishing it with the finest appointments available. It was described in the 1862 local papers as "in apple-pie order and worth the price at $7 per week. . . ."

McCully House, one of six buildings original to Jacksonville, is on the National Registry of Historic Places. The Greek Revival home is graceful in its simplicity. Innkeeper Fran Wing, a design consultant for commercial interiors, emulates the subdued elegance of the columned exterior in her treatment of the parlors and guest rooms.

Rooms are painted in soft, understated colors, providing a quiet backdrop for introducing modern touches into the historic space. Contemporary bleached-oak chairs and tables in the dining room blend smoothly with a square grand piano, original to the house, and the Victorian furnishings. A black walnut Renaissance bedroom suite, ordered by the McCully's and shipped round the horn for their new mansion, is still in place in the master bedroom.

Lending a contemporary aesthetic to the décor are several dozen lithographs by Oregon artist Jon Jay, who is strongly influenced by Oriental art. Several of the pieces are housed in handmade painted boxes with hinged doors that allow opening or closing.

MCCULLY HOUSE INN. 240 East California Street, P.O. Box 387, Jacksonville, OR 97530; (503) 899-1942; Fran and Hal Wing, hosts. Four rooms, each with private bath. Rates: $65. Off-season and mid-week discounts. Includes a full breakfast with fruits, variety of egg dishes, breads, and fine blended coffees. In the heart of Jacksonville, 15 minutes drive from Ashland. Children are welcome; no pets; no smoking; Visa/MasterCard.

DIRECTIONS: from I-5 going north or south, take Jacksonville exit. Once in town, McCully House is clearly marked on the corner of the main street of town.

LIVINGSTON MANSION

The romance of history

Built high on a rise overlooking the foothills of the Siskiyou Mountains and the valley of the Rouge River, Livingston Mansion affords a spectacular view of Jacksonville and the surrounding terrain. From the cool depths of its western-style, paneled living room, where a fire crackles on the massive stone hearth, to the contemporary, sun-spangled swimming pool, visitors feel the romantic heritage of a historic locale.

Gold was discovered in the area in 1852, and the village attracted wealth and commerce. For a time, Jacksonville was the largest town in southern Oregon. Designated a National Historic District, today it is a monument to western history. Visitors enjoy strolling through the charming streets, where meticulously restored buildings echo the past.

Guest rooms are bright and expansive. The blue and white Amour suite has richly carved Belgian furniture and French doors leading to a charming bath with clawfoot tub and old-fashioned ring shower. The mauve and burgundy Regal suite has a fireplace, touches of paisley, and louvered doors between the rooms, making the suite suitable for families.

LIVINGSTON MANSION, 4132 Livingston Road, P.O. Box 1476, Jacksonville, OR 97530; (503) 899-7107; Wally and Sherry Lossing, hosts. Three rooms, all with private baths. Rates: $65 and $75. Includes full breakfast that often includes fresh fruit and ice cream, eggs Benedict or crêpes, breads and "breakfast cookies." Business rates. Families welcome; no pets; smoking permitted in the living room and on outside patio only; Visa/ MasterCard. Sheba is the dog in residence. Swimming pool and small pond.

DIRECTIONS: from I-5 take the Medford exit and proceed west on Rte. 238. Go through Jacksonville and take a right onto North Oregon St. Continue about a mile to Livingston, take a left, and follow to the top of the hill.

UNDER THE GREENWOOD TREE

Fanciful and carefree

In Shakespeare's comedy *As You Like It*, living "Under the Greenwood Tree" refers to retreating into the forest to live in the home of shepherds and milk maids. This romantic, carefree notion describes the atmosphere of Renate Ellam's country estate. This secluded, two-story yellow farmhouse is shaded by magnificent century-old oak trees adorned with colorful hanging kites. Begging to be explored are adjacent handhewn, hand-pegged buildings dating back to 1861: a three-story cavernous old barn, a carriage house filled with original farm tools, wagons, and plows, and a still-operating ten-ton weigh station for weighing hay wagons.

As guests explore the farm, they should acquaint themselves with *all* its residents: Henrietta, the third most beautiful donkey in Jackson County (she ate the ribbons that prove it), and Harvey, the white angora rabbit. Pigeons, partridges, pheasant, and doves are plentiful, and a pair of Bartlett finches add to the pastoral charm.

Greenwood is a gentleman's farm where luxury prevails. The décor and furnishings are first class, and no measure of comfort has been spared. A collection of crystal decanters, antique Meissen dolls, pieces of Rosenthal china, and an heirloom wedding cup dating back four centuries exemplify Renate's fine taste. In the guest rooms, down comforters, leather bound books by Emily Dick-

A ten ton weigh station from Civil War days that still works.

inson, Lord Byron, and Robert Louis Stevenson, and often an oil painting or an intricate needlepoint chair add character. The sounds of Strauss waltzes frequently premeate the house.

Breakfasts are abundant, with Renate's orange muffins notoriously popular. Afternoon high teas bring rave reviews, and in the evening, cookies and sherry set on a hand-embroidered cloth bid guests to "Go to sleep like the flowers."

UNDER THE GREENWOOD TREE, 3045 Bellinger Lane, Medford, OR 97501; (503) 776-0000; Renate Ellam, host. Four beautifully appointed rooms with private baths. Rates: $65 to $75 May 15 through October 15; $55 to $65 balance of year. Includes full country-fresh breakfast and high tea at 4:30 P.M. Two miles from historic Jacksonville, the 1855 gold rush town, and 10 miles from Ashland. Children over 13 welcome; no pets although horses can be stabled (ample riding ring); smoking permitted on porches; Visa/MasterCard.

DIRECTIONS: from the south on I-5, exit 27, Barnett Road; turn left onto overpass, and turn left at first signal onto Stewart. Follow three miles until it becomes Hull. Continue on Hull one block and turn right onto Bellinger Lane. From the north on I-5, exit 27, Barnett Road;

Left, Demay Pringle, with part of her fabulous doll collection

PRINGLE HOUSE

Fantasy land for doll collectors

Sharing Pringle House with guests are several thousand others, but they don't mind the company because it gives them a chance to show off. Some are 150 years old and come from as far away as Venice, while others are brand new and as American as Shirley Temple! Demay Pringle was a professional doll dresser and restorer when suddenly, a few years ago, a client decided to sell its collection. Voila! A seed was planted and Demay's dolls now number in the thousands. The oldest belonged to a friend's great grandmother; the tallest is papier maché and stands four feet high; the most fascinating is an Eskimo doll with red boots made from reindeer, with elaborate beading. This one is the most loved—well that's hard to say with so many Raggedy Ann's and Kewpies to choose among.

Dolls aren't all that Demay and Jim collect. China plates depicting American schoolhouses pay tribute to Jim's career as a music teacher and numerous framed prints of Irish bagpipers displaying family tartans acknowledge an Irish Heritage. There are photographs on display of every owner of this Victorian from the first owner in 1893 to the present, and in Jim's office are photographic memorabilia from his youth when he was in Hollywood's famed "Movie Choir."

Each of the rooms is filled with an abundance of Victoriana from doilies to dainty antiques, homemade quilts and thoughtful amenities. Guests are welcome to help themselves to coffee and tea throughout the day.

PRINGLE HOUSE, 114 N.E. 7th Street, P.O. Box 578, Oakland, OR 97462: (503) 459-5038: Jim and Demay Pringle, hosts. Two rooms share one bath. Rates $30 to $35. Includes a continental breakfast, often of freshly baked goods. Older children only; no pets; smoking on porches; no credit cards. Johann and Poppin are the cats in residence. One hour south of Eugene.

DIRECTIONS: from the south on I-5, exit at Rte. 138 and proceed 1½ miles to Locust Street, the main street in town, and take a right. The house is straight ahead. From the north on I-5, exit at Rte. 138 and proceed 1½ miles to Locust and take a left.

JOHNSON HOUSE

Turn-of-the-century charm

Built in 1892, this is purported to be the oldest house in Florence. Much of its original wooden trim and detailing remain intact. Although the interior has undergone major restoration, the square symmetrical parlor and dining room have been retained.

Turn-of-the-century furnishings throughout, coupled with accents of lace, freshly cut flowers, and old sepia portraits, add to the house's charm. Included in the stay is a full breakfast of fresh fruits with cream, omelets, an assortment of breads, or Grand Marnier French toast.

Once a prosperous logging town, today Florence is a bustling summertime tourist town, with an expanse of oceanside sand dunes for wonderful beachcombing.

JOHNSON HOUSE, 216 Maple Street, P.O. Box 1892, Florence, OR 97439; (503) 997-8000; Jayne and Ronald Fraese, owners. French spoken by the Fraeses. Five rooms, one with private bath. Rates: $45 to $55. Includes a full breakfast. No children under fourteen; no pets; no smoking; no credit cards.

DIRECTIONS: from US-101, turn west onto Maple street approximately 2 blocks north of the bridge over the Siuslaw River.

McGILLIVRAY'S LOG HOME

Pancakes hot off the wood stove

For forty years Evelyn and Dick McGillivray dreamed of living in a log house. Finally that dream came true, when with vision and ingenuity they drew up plans and together masterminded an extraordinary log home.

Dick himself peeled the bark off hundreds of huge, hand picked Oregon fir, spruce, cedar, oak and pine. It took two years to build this dream house where sixteen foot beams, fourteen inches in diameter, create a setting Paul Bunyan could have considered home. The split log open staircase, the high cathedral ceiling and rustic stone wall separating the living room wood stove from the fine Langwood cooking stove combine to make McGillivray's a very special place indeed.

Being a guest at the McGillivrays is assuredly wonderful, and breakfast is amazing. Evelyn gets the fire in the stove up to perfect temperature and then, using an antique square pancake griddle, produces the best pancakes ever created. Crushed filberts blended into honey butter and a topping made with berries from the garden, almost pre-empt the warm maple syrup.

One young visitor asked his hosts with envy and disbelief, "Do you get to live here all the time?"

McGILLIVRAY'S LOG HOME, 88680 Evers Road, Elmira, OR 97437; (503) 935-3564; Dick & Evelyn McGillivray, hosts. Three rooms, two with private baths; third is a sleeping loft with twin beds that shares a bath. Rates: $40 to $50. Includes lovingly prepared full breakfast and refreshments and cheese in the afternoon. Children are welcome; no pets; smoking on porches; no credit cards. Handicap access.

DIRECTIONS: from Eugene take Rte. 126 west to Elmira. Proceed 2 miles and turn right onto Evers Road. After the fifth house on left, look for black and white pole with log bird house on top that marks the dirveway.

Natural Pacific Northwest landscaping at its best.

MARJON

Kaleidoscope of color

A path meandering through ferns and over a wooden foot bridge leads to the placid waters of the McKenzie River. Along the way there is a dock for sunbathing and rafts for more adventurous activity. Several spots are inviting to those wishing to relax with some reading or early morning coffee. Over seven hundred rhododendrons and two thousand azaleas provide the colorful background for an extraordinary sculpted acre of trees, shrubs, and flowers. From the tall, century-old apple tree, grafted to have nonconcurrent blooming cycles, to the seven varieties of violets, everything is arranged to provide continuous color throughout spring and summer.

Margie Haas, Marjon's hostess, is as imaginative and dramatic as her landscape. A forest scene with white spruces and life-size deer in the corner of her living room creates the kind of spectacle that only hints at Margie's decorating flair. The living room and dining room are appropriately decorated for the season—leprechauns for St. Patrick's Day, flags and Uncle Sam's top hats on the Fourth of July. Halloween presents special opportunities.

The contemporary house has marvelous river views from windows that tower to twenty-one foot high ceilings and extend along half the sixty foot living room. The master suite opens on to the river on one side and to a formal Japanese garden on the other. French Provincial furniture accented with red velvet, a furry white love seat, and pink sunken tub contribute to this suite's extravagance.

MARJON, 44975 Leaburg Dam Road, Leaburg, OR 97489; (503) 896-3145; Margie Haas, host. Two rooms, both with private baths. Rates: $60 to $80. Includes five-course gourmet breakfast, including hand-sculpted fruit served under a glass dome, cheeses, breads, and eggs. No children; no pets; no smoking in the bedrooms; Visa/MasterCard.

DIRECTIONS: from Eugene take Rte. 126 East for 24 miles. Turn right onto Leaburg Dam Road which crosses over the top of the dam. Proceed for one mile; the road ends at Marjon.

MADISON INN

A family affair

Aided by six offspring who are responsible for everything from bookkeeping to cooking, Kathryn Brandis has created an open and relaxing guest house in her gracious, gabled home.

Perhaps the main reason for the genial atmosphere at the Madison Inn is Kathryn's genius with people. Explains eldest son Matthew: "Mom is incredible. She knows a little something about almost everything and can always spur interesting conversation around the breakfast table."

The spectacular woodwork, moldings, and architectural detail of the house warrant its entry on the National Historic Register.

Located across from a quiet park, the Madison Inn is convenient to both Oregon State University and downtown Corvallis. But the real attraction of the inn is the warmth and hospitality of the Brandis clan.

MADISON INN, 660 SW Madison, Corvallis, OR 97333; (503) 757-1274; Kathryn Brandis, owner; Paige, Matthew, Honore, Mike, Shannon, and Kathleen Brandis, deputy hosts. Spanish and French spoken. Five rooms, one with private bath, the remaining four rooms sharing two baths. Rate: $45. Includes full breakfast of baked eggs, English muffins, and blended fruit juices. Children welcome; no pets; Raggs is the household dog.

DIRECTIONS: from I-5, take the Corvallis-Oregon State exit. Go west ten miles, cross over bridge and take a left onto 6th. Go three blocks, take a right onto Madison, and continue to 7th.

Beautifully preserved woodwork reflects the character of this 1903 Queen Anne.

CAMPUS COTTAGE

Unpretentious charm near Fraternity Row

Campus Cottage is a cozy frame bungalow tucked along the border of the University of Oregon's beautiful campus. Situated among the sprawling structures of Fraternity Row, the inn is ideally located for visitors to the university and is minutes away from downtown Eugene.

The original master bedroom, The Suite, has a brass bedstead and its own sitting room; the cozy Guest Room has an antique oak bed and down-cushioned reading chair. Guests are invited to curl up in the parlor in front of the fire or work on the house jigsaw puzzle. Bicycles are furnished for those wanting to pedal their way around town or campus.

Innkeeper Ursula Bates, herself an experienced traveler, waxes enthusiastic about the pleasures of bed and breakfast inns. Committed to starting each day with a nourishing meal, she serves guests a variety of breakfast foods, from baked egg dishes and fresh fruits to hot breads and beverages. Ursula is a knowledgeable guide to her city and is especially proud of the new Hult Center for the Performing Arts, the fine selection of French restaurants, and the Fifth Street Public Market, which is Eugene's answer to San Francisco's Ghirardelli Square.

CAMPUS COTTAGE, 1136 East 19th Avenue, Eugene, OR 97403; (503) 342-5346; Ursula Bates, proprietress; Susan Stevens, hostess. Three rooms. Rates: $65 to $78. Includes a full breakfast with a variety of baked egg dishes, fresh fruits. Older children only; no pets; no credit cards. Cats Gus and Lizzie and Annie, the dog, in residence.

DIRECTIONS: from the south on I-5, exit at 192 which becomes Franklin Blvd. Take a left at the third light onto Agate St., following signs to the University of Oregon. Turn right onto 19th St. and go 3½ blocks.

GENERAL HOOKER'S HOUSE

Portland Victorian

In one corner of the parlor, there is a spinning wheel—Lorry Hall, the hostess dyes and spins her own wool. The Victorian home, named after Civil War General "Fighting Joe" Hooker, is decorated in contemporary fashion with white walls and tan canvas furnishings combined with natural rattan, formica, and chrome. Chandeliers and lighted stained glass cast a bejeweled aura. Lori's love of travel is evident from the batik quilts and curtains she picked up on one of her journeys.

The view of downtown Portland from the second story sundeck is wondrous by day and magical by night. The neighborhood is residential, with nearby parks and tennis courts, yet only minutes from the business district by bus, car, or on foot.

GENERAL HOOKER'S HOUSE, 125 SW Hooker, Portland, OR 97201; (503) 222-4435; Lorry Hall, host. Three rooms, one with private bath. Rates: $45 to $60. Includes continental breakfast. No children under 14; no pets; Visa/MasterCard/American Express. Metro "Y" one block away with indoor track, so bring your membership card if you belong to a YMCA. Ten minutes south of downtown Portland.

DIRECTIONS: from the south on I-5; take Corbutt Street exit. Take the left ramp over I-5 and then make a left onto Hamilton. Bear right onto Barbur Blvd. In approx. one mile, the Metro Y will be on your far left; take a right onto SW Hooker.

Built high on the rocky shore overlooking this inlet, Channel House commands a magnificent view of all nautical comings-and-goings. A modern, shingled structure, the inn was designed with the sea in mind, and the most desirable accommodations are those that face the water. With sliding glass doors that open onto private balconies, these rooms make guests feel as if they have set to sea. Two of the large oceanfront suites, equipped with full kitchens, working fireplaces, and whirlpool baths, are perfect for two couples traveling together.

Breakfast can be enjoyed in the first-floor restaurant, decorated with an array of antique brass ships' fittings, or in the privacy of one's room. In the restaurant, a CB radio picks up fishing news from the nearby boats. Charter boats, equipped for a day of serious fishing or for a pleasure cruise, are available at the harbor.

CHANNEL HOUSE

Endless nautical views

Carved by nature from the rugged Oregon coastline, Depoe Bay is a calm and picturesque body of water favored by sport and commercial fishermen alike. However, navigators pay their dues in the channel that connects the bay to the sea. Nicknamed "The Jaws," it is a treacherous inlet that commands the respect of the most stalwart old salt.

CHANNEL HOUSE, P.O. Box 56, Depoe Bay, OR 97341; (503) 765-2140; Paul Schwabe, owner. Seven rooms, each with private bath, two of which are large oceanfront suites with full kitchens, fireplaces and whirlpools. Rates: $35 to $120. Includes full continental breakfast. Children are welcome, as are well-behaved pets by previous arrangement.

DIRECTIONS: located on the coast between Newport and Lincoln. Turn west at supermarket onto Ellingson St., just south of the bridge over Depoe Bay.

Perched right on the ocean, you can have breakfast in your room and look at the ever-changing view. Left, Depoe Bay, an Oregon coastal town.

WHITE HOUSE

A majestic mansion aptly named

Built in 1910 in what was once a resort area for the Portland elite, this grand house belonged to a rags-to-riches lumber tycoon. The mansion, airy and elegantly proportioned, suited his wife's desire to live in a bright and expansive home instead of a dark Victorian-style house prevalent at the time.

Because it closely resembles the president's home in Washington, D.C., neighbors have aptly nicknamed the 7,600 square foot mansion the "White House." The colossal classic portico with six Doric columns is reminiscent of southern plantation manors. French arched transoms with amber glass, a second-story curved balustrade balcony, and a Mediterranean red tile roof add contrast to the classic style.

Owners Larry and Mary Hough.

Details in the entrance hall, right, and the stairway, above, provide a stunning welcome.

The interior is equally dramatic. Graciously tall windows and twelve-foot-high cove ceilings are trimmed with Honduran mahogany. A grand staircase with four stained-glass windows at the landing adds special magnificence.

Hand-painted wall murals in the front entrance depict rural scenes which recall the grounds at the turn of the century. The huge living room, dining room, and downstairs ballroom indicate the grand entertaining which took place within their walls.

Innkeepers Larry and Mary Hough handle the grandeur with cheery aplomb. Dublin born, Mary was brought up in an English boardinghouse and takes to hostessing quite naturally. Larry enjoys the challenge of the ongoing restoration and clearly enjoys the guests. Theirs is a happy home where visitors are indulged in luxury and jovial, warm hospitality.

WHITE HOUSE, 1914 N.E. 22nd Avenue, Portland, OR 97212; (503) 287-7131; Larry and Mary Hough, hosts. Six rooms, two with private baths. Rates: $37 to $60. Includes a full breakfast that varies between eight different English style menus that may include scones, soda bread, oatmeal, and cooked fruits. Children under 12 discouraged; no pets; no smoking; Visa/MasterCard. Seven minutes from downtown business district.

DIRECTIONS: from the north on I-5, take the Coliseum exit. Proceed straight and make a left onto Weildler Blvd. Go to 22nd Ave and turn left. From the south on I-5, take a right onto Weildler Blvd. Go to 22nd Ave and turn left.

Left, the front parlor, which gets a lot of use.

WILLIAM'S HOUSE

All the comforts of home

The rugged beauty of the Columbia River Gorge, with Mt. Adams and Mt. Hood ever present, has attracted generations. Today, acres of cherry and apple orchards, hiking trails, fishing, wind surfing, and endlessly beautiful vistas add to its unique appeal. The Williams family came to this community, at the end of the Oregon Trail, in 1867 and, by selling wagon provisions to the pioneering settlers, built a retailing empire.

Don and Barbara Williams enjoy sharing the home that has been in their family since 1926. On a hillside next to Mill Creek, the Williams House is an oversized beautiful 1899 Victorian.

A welcoming and spacious front porch, a gazebo adjacent to a kitchen, and two distinctive second story porches—one a belvedere tower—make the home charming. Georgian and Victorian antiques are highlighted against vibrant red carpeting. An oil painting depicting an equestrian scene of a young woman off to a hunt, riding a luminescent Arabian stallion, hangs over the piano in the living room. An early nineteenth century Viole de Gambe and a collection of antique oriental porcelain are not to be missed. This is a place that feels lived in, and at the same time offers a comfortable elegance.

WILLIAM'S HOUSE, 608 West 6th Street, The Dalles, OR 97058; (503) 296-2889; Don & Barbara Williams, hosts. Three rooms, one with private bath; two with balconies with views of Klickitat Hills. Rates: $45 to $55. Inquire about commercial, mid-week discount. Includes breakfast, beginning with homemade granola, fresh fruits, yogurts, and muffins. Telephones and television on request. Well-behaved children welcome; no pets; smoking in the parlors; Visa/MasterCard. Wonderful maps of self-guided driving tours are provided as well as Don's personal tips on the best places with the best views!

DIRECTIONS: from the west, take Rte. 84 at exit 83. Turn left at stop sign to West 6th St. Cross Trevitt St. and just across the bridge, the house is on the right.

WASHINGTON

INN OF THE WHITE SALMON

Where good taste prevails

This is the place to come for breakfast and to stay several extra days—that is, if you want to taste everything. Both pastry chef and innkeeper, Loretta Hopper serves more than forty different items daily. Pastries, cakes, breads, and tarts are freshly baked with an assist from two other bakers, and there are orange cream-cheese rolls, pear frangipane, cinnamon toast, flan, Danish bread dough with an almond paste filling, and tart Mirabelle with kirsch-soaked prunes. All are beautiful to behold and incredibly delicious. Since there are six different egg dishes in addition to everything else, it is impossible to try everything at even two or three breakfasts.

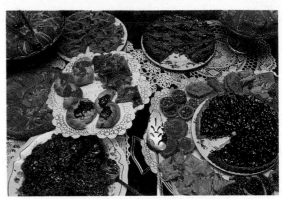

Some of the 42 breakfast treats.

INN OF THE WHITE SALMON, 172 W. Jewett, White Salmon, WA 98672; (509) 493-2335; Loretta and Bill Hopper, owners. Nina Benge, manager. Twenty rooms, nineteen with private bath, furnished with period antiques in two-story 1930s brick building. Rates: $78 to $126. Includes an extraordinary breakfast of fresh pastries and gourmet egg dishes. Well-supervised children welcome; no pets; smoking permitted but not in dining room; Visa/MasterCard/American Express. Hot tub. Located in the fabulously beautiful Columbia River gorge.

DIRECTIONS: east of Portland on I-84, for 64 miles to exit 64. Follow signs to White Salmon; the inn is towards the end of town on the right.

Above, Loretta Hopper, hostess and pastry chef.

HAUS ROHRBACH PENSION

Bavarian-style pension

Leavenworth is a reincarnated Bavarian village in the moutainous region of central Washington. From the five porches and decks of Haus Rohrbach, guests have a sweeping vista of the valley and mountains beyond. At night, the view from the balconies of the inn shows the shimmering lights of the town, which cast a magic spell over the valley.

Haus Rohrbach's guest rooms provide simple pleasures: a bit of stenciling, stained pine wainscoting, handmade benches and counter tops, a couple of hooks and a pine shelf with a rod serving as a closet. What is wonderful here is cuddling under down-filled comforters, breathing the fresh mountain air, and listening to the birds and coyotes as the night falls.

The common rooms are large and lodge-like, with built-in benches and long tables for breakfast. There is even a large, carpeted room designated for younger family members. Plenty of coffee, tea, cider, and, sometimes, special sundaes and strudels can be purchased from the Haus kitchen after days of sledding, skiing, horseback riding, or hiking.

HAUS ROHRBACH PENSION, 12882 Ranger Road, Leavenworth, WA 98826; (509) 548-7024; Kathryn & Bob Harrild, hosts; Twelve rooms, three with private baths. Rustic, simple decor with fluffy down comforters. Rates: $55 to $65. Includes fabulous breakfast of house specialties such as puffed sourdough pancakes with jams made of local berries. Children are welcome; no pets; smoking in common rooms and on balconies; Visa/MasterCard. Spa open all year; pool is opened for season. Two alpine goats and a family duck roam the lawns.

DIRECTIONS: from Rte. 2 turn onto Ski Hill Drive. Go one mile and turn left onto Ranger Road. Follow straight ahead to Pension.

BROWN'S FARM

A rustic, rural retreat

A few miles from town, the pine pole log home is tucked into a clearing in the woods. From the wrap-around porch, you can see the farm's horses, goats, chickens, sheep, rabbits, cats, and dogs. Wendi and Steve and the younger Browns are full of tales about the animals, proud to share with travelers the country pleasures of this quiet and unpretentious retreat. Inside the farmhouse there is a large grey hearth lovingly created with stones from the nearby Icicle River Valley. Rag rugs and lots of overstuffed furniture with colorful crocheted throws invite guests to kick off their shoes and curl up for a while.

Heirloom quilts hang on the walls along with other collected Victorian and country memorabilia. Framed in the hall are a dozen or so fascinating labels from the region's apple packing companies that artistically portray local scenes of orchards, mountains, rivers, and wildlife.

After a hearty breakfast of Wendi's inch-thick French toast or Steve's four-star omelets served to guests from the country kitchen, guests can explore the miles of hiking trails through the woods or browse through dozens of shops in the nearby Bavarian village of Leavenworth.

BROWN'S FARM, 11150 Highway 209, Leavenworth, WA 98826; Wendi and Steve Brown, hosts. (509) 548-7863; Two rooms with shared bath. Rates: $55 to $60. Includes full country breakfast of French toast and sausage or gourmet omelets. Children welcome (bring sleeping bag and pillow); no pets; no smoking in guest rooms; Visa/MasterCard. Family members, Emily, Jennifer, and Peter, are around to share stories, or to help with babysitting for a small fee.

DIRECTIONS: from Seattle on Rte. 2, turn left onto Rte. 209. Continue for 1½ miles. The sign is on the right; the driveway on the left. Keep to the left and the driveway will end at the farmhouse.

Modeled after a 15th-century English inn, and reproduced in authentic detail.

THE SWAN INN

Sample the fifteenth century

After spending their honeymoon at the Crown Inn of Chiddingfold, Surrey, England, and falling in love with it, Richard and Jeri Bain decided to re-create it. Eleven years ago, they built this fifteenth-century English Tudor inn on an island of farmhouses. Set back in the woods at the end of a long driveway, the Swan Inn is startling to come upon.

After drawing up plans, the Bains worked with Australian Peter Crocker, a local contractor who was familiar with Tudor architecture. Cedar beam construction dating back a thousand years, leaded and stained-glass windows imported from abroad, and rustic old iron hardware all help to duplicate an authentic fifteenth-century inn. Crossing the threshold, one finds an entrance paved with old

bricks, a 1790 English clock, and a Jacobean table from the 1600s.

Richard Bain is a dedicated preindustrialist, fascinated with the literature, philosophy, and life-styles of the fourteenth, fifteenth, and sixteenth centuries. The Swan Inn is filled with objects he has collected, including brass rubbings of a 1451 Flemish knight, a chest carved in 1606, a flintlock British musket dating from 1798, dozens of horse brasses, and an impressive array of other antique furnishings and treasures. Upstairs in a guest room, there is an oval mirror recessed into the foot of an ornate bed, which Richard explains was used by ladies to check their hemlines.

THE SWAN INN, Route 5, Box 454, Vashon, Vashon Island, WA 98070; (206) 463-3388; Jeri and Richard Bain, owners. Three rooms decorated in 15th- to 18th-century English furnishings with either a private or shared bath. Rates: $55 to $75. Includes an expanded continental breakfast week-days and a full breakfast weekends. Children over eight; no pets; Visa/MasterCard. Hiking trails go through surrounding woods, and the beach is 15 minutes away. Pool, tennis, and 9-hole golf course nearby.

DIRECTIONS: Vashon Island is a 15-minute ferry ride from West Seattle. From I-5, follow signs for Vashon Ferry which leaves from Fauntleroy Way. Take the main road to Vashon from either ferry dock, turn west at the stop light and follow Bank Road (SW 176th street). Watch for a blue mailbox No. 454 and "Swan Inn" sign.

Dusk is a beautiful time at the farm.

THE MANOR FARM INN

A gentleman's farm

Grazing around the Manor Farm Inn's 1886 two-story white farmhouse are dozens of border Cheviot sheep, long-haired tan Highland cattle, and a herd of Guernsey cows. There are well-groomed horses in the barn and ducks around the pond, which was recently stocked with ten thousand rainbow trout. The twenty-five acres of rolling green meadows surrounding this century-old inn are punctuated by stark white wooden fences.

A rose-covered veranda leads from the parlor, past the guest rooms, and into the dining room. Hors d'oeuvres and sherry are served by the fire in the parlor, furnished with a good sampling of country pine antiques. The dining room's pine chairs were made in Appalachia. At tables covered with pink and white handwoven linens, a gourmet dinner is served by candlelight with classical music in the background. Roast quail, lobster, or flank steak in a plum-pear sauce can be one of the entrées in a five-course meal, and dinner is often completed with port and cheese three hours later.

The meals are prepared by host Robin Hughes, a former restaurateur. Robin believes that guests should encounter an entirely restorative experience here, consisting of elegant surroundings, enticing food, and exquisite serenity. A gentleman's farm, such as this, can provide these pleasures.

THE MANOR FARM INN, 26069 Big Valley Road, N.E., Poulsbo, WA 98370; (206) 779-4628; Robin and Jill Hughes, hosts. Ten guest rooms furnished with French country antiques, each with private bath and several with fireplaces. Rates: $50 to $85. Includes wake-up coffee brought to the room and lavish country breakfast in the dining room a bit later. Sherry and hors d'oeuvres served in the parlor. Hot tub available. No children; no pets; no smoking; Visa/MasterCard. Gourmet dinners with fixed price are served in the restaurant at one seating. Entire working farm open for guests' pleasure.

DIRECTIONS: from Seattle, take the Winslow Ferry and follow signs to Polsbo (Rte. 305). In Polsbo, continue following signs to Hood Canal Bridge. Just before the bridge take Rte. 3 south towards Lofall. Follow signs to Kitsap Memorial State Park and proceed until a large sign for Manor Farm Inn marks the turn onto Big Valley Road, NE.

The graceful interior of a fine house.

CHAMBERED NAUTILUS

A stately structure

The Chambered Nautilus is a classic colonial structure situated high on a hill in Seattle's university district. With elegant white columns flanking the entryway and supporting the graceful sun porch, the home is at once stately and gracious.

Both the first-floor living room and adjoining dining room, where innkeepers Deborah Sweet and Kate McDill serve breakfast, are equipped with working fireplaces. Breakfast might include homemade breads, waffles, fresh fruits, yogurt, or a savory quiche. One bite of Kate's buttery scones, rich coffee cakes, and feather-light muffins reveals her expertise as a baker.

Each of the large and airy bedrooms is furnished with thoughtfully coordinated beds and bureaus, and several rooms open onto private porches that overlook the ivy-covered hillside and colorful gardens. Throughout, contemporary graphic prints and delicate watercolors decorate the walls.

After breakfast, visitors may spend the day exploring the pleasures of Seattle and the sur-

rounding area. Deborah is an avid runner who can guide guests to the best running paths in the neighborhood.

CHAMBERED NAUTILUS, 5005 22nd Avenue, N.E., Seattle, WA 98105; (206) 522-2536; Kate McDill and Deborah Sweet, hosts. Six rooms with three shared baths. Rates: $45 to $70. Includes full breakfast of scones, muffins or coffee cake, fresh fruits and yogurts, quiche, waffles, and baked egg dishes. Children under twelve by special arrangement; no pets; smoking in living room only; all major credit cards. The dog of the house, Keri, is a shy white Samoyed. Dinners, wine tastings, and other special events can be accommodated. The house is accessible only by a flight of steps.

DIRECTIONS: from I-5, take 50th St. East exit. Proceed about 1½ miles and turn left onto 20th Ave. N.E. Go four blocks and take a right onto 54th St. N.E. Proceed down a steep hill and turn right onto 22nd St. N.E.

Left, the large Corner Suite has its own deck.

SHUMWAY MANSION

Mobile mansion in the woods

Some people move mountains. Others move mansions! This 10,000 square foot estate was literally picked up from its original site and three days, several traffic jams, and $100,000 later, gently placed on its new foundation on a hillside above Juanita Bay. Dick Harris, a stock broker whose hobby was masterminding the relocating of buildings, commented with absolute resolve, "I've moved twenty-nine buildings, but this is the last!"

The impressive grey shingled 1909 four story home, reminiscent of Eastern coastal mansions, was destined for demolition, if not for Dick and Salli Harris's vision. Salli, who is fondly referred to as "Mrs. Wedding of Seattle", has been in the business of planning weddings and receptions for most of her career. She and Dick looked at fifty homes before deciding on this one as having the perfect ambiance and setting for both social affairs and unusual lodging. The expansive grace of the living room, the mirrored paneling in the dining room, an enclosed sun porch, and several smaller parlors offered the elegance and grandeur they sought. With the enthusiastic support of the local community, the dream to preserve and restore this beautifully built home became a reality. Three and one-half miles of new wiring and eleven bathrooms later, the Inn was born. Today Shumway stands ready to welcome travelers into this new chapter of its history.

SHUMWAY MANSION, 11410 100th Avenue, N.E., Kirkland, WA 98033; (206) 823-2303; Julie Blakemore, host; Dick and Salli Harris, owners. Seven rooms, each with private bath; five with view of Lake Washington; two have balconies. Rates: $57.50 to $62.50. Includes a full breakfast. Children over 12; no pets; smoking in public rooms; Visa/MasterCard. Privileges at Juanita Bay Athletic Club. 25 minutes from downtown Seattle. Luncheons and weddings are catered regularly.

DIRECTIONS: from the south on I-405, take N.E. 116th St. at exit 20A; go west under the freeway; one block before stoplight turn left on 99th Place N.E. (99 becomes 100th) From the north on I-405, take N.E. 124th St. at exit 20; turn left on 116th Avenue, N.E. Turn right onto N.E. 116th Street; one block before stoplight turn left onto 99th Place N.E.

GUEST HOUSE BED & BREAKFAST

Rustic choices

Situated on twenty-five acres of wooded property, Guest House offers several different styles of accommodations. Capturing the traditional flavor of a bed and breakfast inn, a one-story farmhouse contains two guest rooms, with antique furnishings, country quilts, shared bath, family-style dining room, and snug living room and fireplace. Behind that main farmhouse is a bright yellow one-room guest cottage, with a wide porch and knotty pine interior.

Bordering on a reflecting pond are the Carriage House, a sizable cabin in the woods with a skylight over the bed, and the Log Cabin, which is smaller and more rustic. Built of logs, it has a cozy sleeping loft, kitchen, and sitting area.

The most luxurious accommodation is the Lodge, a large two-story log home with a deck that reaches to the edge of the pond. Its appointments are classic: a massive stone fireplace, a moose head over the mantel, heavy wooden doors with iron latches.

GUEST HOUSE BED & BREAKFAST, 835 E. Christenson Road, Greenbank, Whidby Island, WA 98253; (206) 678-3115; Don and Mary Jane Creger, hosts. Three cottages and a lodge, all with private baths, kitchens, and fireplaces or wood stoves. Wildflower suite in the farmhouse with private bath. Rates: $55 to $125. Includes a full self-serve breakfast of cereals, muffins or croissant, and boiled eggs. No children under fourteen; no pets;.no smoking; Visa/MasterCard. Swimming pool and hot tub on grounds.

DIRECTIONS: from Whidbey Island/Mukilteo Ferry, drive 16 miles on Rte. 525. At Christenson Rd. there are signs for "The Guest House."

The solarium, sun deck, and hot tub are discreetly tucked out of sight.

CAROLINE'S COUNTRY COTTAGE

Formerly a farmhouse

Caroline's Country Cottage is a snug and tidy farmhouse blessed with a wonderful view of the distant Cascade Mountains, the calm waters of the Saratoga Passage, and the tiny town of Langley.

The living room is decorated in soothing shades of sea green, soft colors that blend with the scenery and complement the handsome lines of the hearth. The three guest bedrooms are decorated in a harmonious blend of pastel fabrics, cozy comforters, and bright garden flowers.

A solar heated sun room with floor to ceiling glass envelopes like a green house and offers panoramic views of the Cascade Mountains. Outdoors a gazebo has been built on an acre of wild flowers—lupine, daisies, snapdragons, foxglove. Visitors are invited to stroll about the three acres of manicured grounds and amble through the raised-bed garden, where a profusion of grapes, berries, herbs, and vegetables thrive in this temperate climate.

CAROLINE'S COUNTRY COTTAGE, 215 6th Street, P.O. Box 459, Langley, Whidbey Island, WA 98260; (206) 221-8709; Jack and Caroline Satterberg, owners. Three bedrooms with private baths. Rates: $75. Includes full breakfast with egg dish, sausage, muffins, and berries from the garden. No children; no pets; no smoking. One dog ant two cats in residence.

DIRECTIONS: take I-5 to the Whidbey Island/Mukilteo Ferry exit. Take the ferry to Clinton and proceed into Langley on Rte. 525. Turn right on Langley Road, pass the high school on the left and when you come to a Y in the road, take the left fork, which is 6th St.

THE SARATOGA INN

Sophisticated country comfort

On 25 acres overlooking the Saratoga Passage.

Here Chippendale and Queen Anne furnishings mix with country pine and folk art. There is much warmth and whimsy in the décor, along with good taste and sophistication. At the Saratoga Inn the rooms look like pages from an interior design magazine, but they are wholly inviting.

Comfortable couches in the living room beckon you to curl up by the fire with a good book and a cup of tea or glass of wine. A dark blue carpet offsets a bright floral chair. Wooden decoys, a copper weather vane, and painted rocking horse harmonize with an Oriental rug and grandfather clock. A collection of lead soldiers belonging to innkeeper Ted Jones and his son are in a living room cabinet.

Upstairs, the bedrooms are beautifully appointed, with a distinguished collection of hand-made quilts, early American antiques, mono-grammed cotton sheets, and comfortable chairs.

Picture windows offer stunning views of the quaint village of Langley, and large modern bathrooms are filled with a generous selection of sweet-smelling toiletries.

THE SARATOGA INN, 4850 South Coles Road, Langley, Whidbey Island, WA 98260; (206) 221-7526; Debbie and Ted Jones, hosts. Five guest rooms with private baths. Rates $60 to $80. Includes a delicious buffet breakfast. Children under fourteen by special arrangement only; no pets; smoking allowed on the outside porches only. Two cats and a golden retriever in residence. Within walking distance of Langley, a delightful seaside village with several fine shops, galleries, and an excellent theater.

DIRECTIONS: from Seattle, take I-5 north to Whidbey Island/ Mukilteo Ferry exit 189. Take the 15-minute ferry ride to Clinton on Whidbey Island. Proceed into Langley and take Third St., which becomes Brooks Hill Rd. Take a left onto Coles Rd. and the entrance to the inn is on the right.

The soft, cool colors were suggested by the handmade quilt on the wall.

CLIFF HOUSE

An architectural masterpiece

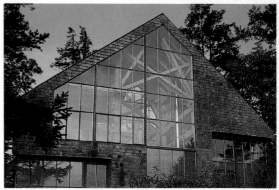

Designed to let in the light, this house captures the imagination.

Cliff House is simply breathtaking! Philip Johnson, the renowned architect who selected Cliff House to receive an AIA award in 1980, was particularly taken with the large open atrium rising through the center of the house and the profusion of natural light that floods the interior. As its name indicates, Cliff House sits on a bluff above the sea—its large windows revealing the drama of the Olympic Mountains in the distance, high above the Admiralty Straights. Ships steaming into Seattle pass offshore, and blood-red sunsets reflecting off the water, make this an unusually romantic and spectacularly beautiful place.

The interior of the house blends rugged stone with cedar structural beams, a luxurious sunken living room, plush carpeting, primitive art, delicate paintings, and nature photographs taken by the hostess, Peggy Moore. Because the house is so much a part of her life, Peggy is exhilarated by her guests' enthusiasm. She rents the one-bedroom house in its entirety, to one couple at a time.

CLIFF HOUSE, 5440 S. Grigware Road, Freeland, WA 98249; (206) 321-1566; Peggy Moore, hostess. The entire house is for rent. One bedroom with king-size bed with ocean view. Rates: $145. Includes continental breakfast. Cannot accommodate children or pets; non-smokers are preferred; no credit cards. Stairway to the beach and hot tub on outside deck in a 13-acre secluded wooded setting.

DIRECTIONS: from the Whidbey Island/Mukilteo Ferry, drive 11 miles on Rte. 525 and turn left onto Bush Point Rd. (after pizza parlor on left and Book Bay on right). Proceed 1¼ miles and turn left on Grigware Rd. The driveway is on the right.

The view of the sea from the king-sized bed is rapturous.

CHANNEL HOUSE

Spectacular views of the San Juan Islands

From the large outdoor hot tub behind this house you can get a panoramic view of the sunset over Puget Sound and the boats navigating the Guemes Channel. Built in 1902, this three-story bungalow is just minutes from the ferry.

Furnished throughout with turn-of-the-century pieces, the guest rooms are large and airy and have antique brass, mahogany, and canopied beds. The main floor will make guests feel perfectly at home. There is a library and music room with its own fireplace, an inviting formal living room, and a tiled solarium filled with all manner of greenery. A full breakfast of fresh fruit, home-baked breads, and an assortment of egg dishes is served in the sunny dining room.

Host Sam Salzinger will offer an invitation, if the weather is good, to join him aboard his twenty-three-foot sailboat. But those who are partial to land can drive through nearby Washington Park to find a sandy beach and spectacular views of the San Juan Islands.

A large French country style barn is on the drawing board, and will house a host of activities, including a variety of art courses and concerts.

CHANNEL HOUSE, 2902 Oakes Avenue, Anacortes, WA 98221. (206) 293-9382. Sam and Kathy Salzinger, hosts. Four rooms with two shared baths. Rates: $45 to $65. Inquire about weekly rates. Includes a full breakfast of fruits, baked breads and egg dishes. No children under twelve; no pets. Smoking is permitted in the common areas but not in the rooms; no credit cards. Outdoor hot tub.

DIRECTIONS: from I-5, take Highway 20 west and follow signs to Anacortes Ferry, which will put you on Oakes Avenue. Follow the numbers to 2902 Oakes and Channel House is on the right, waterside.

Built by an Italian count in 1902.

Painting of the hostess at age seven with her grandfather.

KANGAROO HOUSE

Where quality of life matters

This bungalow-style house combines the romance of living on an island with the fruits of tradition. Brought from the mainland are the fine old cherrywood china closet that belonged to inn-keeper Polly Nisbet's grandmother and the spindled four-poster bed that Polly slept in as a child.

Beautiful aspects of the island are in evidence too: the fieldstone fireplace that was built by the Nesbits with stones from a farmer's field.

Good restaurants, quaint shops, and galleries are to be found on Orcas Island, and there are swimming, fishing, and hiking at nearby Moran State Park.

KANGAROO HOUSE, P.O. Box 334, North Beach Road, Eastsound, Orcas Island, WA 98245; (206) 376-2175; Ken and Polly Nisbet, hosts. Five guest rooms with shared baths. Four with sinks in room. Rates: $45 to $55. Includes a full breakfast of baked eggs, fresh fruits, and baked breads. Children under six by previous arrangement; no pets; smoking permitted in living room only; Visa/MasterCard. Check during January and February as to exact dates of winter closing schedule.

DIRECTIONS: the island can be reached by air from Seattle or via the Washington State Ferry, which has seven departures each day in season from Anacortes and takes about 1¼ hrs. Once on Orcas follow the ferry traffic and the signs into Eastsound. Take a left at the only traffic light onto North Beach Rd. and go about a mile. The house is on the left.

OVERLEAF: *Washington State Ferry arriving at picturesque Orcas Island.*

HASTINGS HOUSE INN

Tower views of Port Townsend

Carefully maintained as a family residence until it became an inn, Hastings House never required restoration, and today it is on the National Register of Historic Landmarks. Built in 1889 by one of the founders of Port Townsend, Frank Hasting's home can be described as a Queen Anne Victorian with an Edwardian influence.

Two elegant turrets, a wraparound porch, a quarter-turn staircase, Italian ceramic fireplaces, hand-rubbed oak woodwork, and an Italian blown glass grape chandelier are original to the house. The old furniture is no longer here, but the house has been decorated with a sensitivity to the period and to its architectural lines and scale. Everything is simple and elegant and looks as if it belongs.

Rising three stories, the turret at the front corner of the house creates delightful circular alcoves in the main floor parlor and in the master and third-floor bedrooms. Each of the upstairs alcoves serves as a charming sitting room for the bedrooms, and each has a marvelous view of Admiralty Inlet.

Bruce and Grace Peirson, who manage this inn, say they "try to keep guests happy and comfortable." Happiness and comfort are just what you'll find.

HASTINGS HOUSE INN, Washington and Walker Streets, Port Townsend, WA 98368; (206) 385-3553; Bruce and Grace Peirson, managers. Seven rooms, including 2 bridal suites; private and shared baths. Rates: $45 to $75. Winter rates slightly less. Includes full breakfast of fruit, cinnamon rolls, bread pudding, and cereals. Children over eight; no pets; no smoking; Visa/MasterCard.

DIRECTIONS: from Seattle take the ferry to Winslow and follow the signs to Hood Canal Bridge. Cross bridge and follow signs to Port Townsend. After the first set of lights turn left onto Washington St. Go one block to the top of the hill and the house is on the corner.

A tower guest room.

LIZZIE'S

It is easy to feel at home

Patti and Bill Wickline, the new owners of Lizzie's, are "people persons" and enjoy talking to guests of an evening or over morning coffee. Recent guests include a husband and wife, both professors from Alaska, a Russian psychologist, and the owner of a 1,000 acre maple sugar farm in Canada. The Wicklines feel they are promoting good international relations via bed and breakfast.

Lizzie's—named after Lizzie Grant, the colorful widow of a Port Townsend sea captain—shines with glistening new paint, plumbing, wiring, sprinklers, bathrooms, and kitchen. The Italianate Victorian building is admirably furnished with Queen Anne chairs, a Victorian leather chesterfield sofa, a brilliant red carpet, and a Knabe grand piano. Silk hangings from the Broadway production of *The Flower Drum Song* hang on either side of a marble fireplace. The inn is not

This 1880s Italianate Victorian is part of Port Townsend's legacy.

pretentious, and it is easy to feel at home here.

Breakfasts are served at a twelve-foot oak table in the kitchen, amid welcome informality. Cast-iron muffin tins, a Chinese bamboo steamer, a wire egg basket, and other cooking utensils hang from a handmade iron pot rack overhead. There is a big old hotel stove with six burners, two ovens, and three broilers that is used to serve up a generous continental breakfast of gingerbread, scones, and coffee cake.

There is also a brand of Lizzie's toiletries. The custom-made apricot soaps and lotions are a trademark. Altogether this is a most pleasant place to visit.

LIZZIE'S, 731 Pierce Street, Port Townsend, WA 98368; (206) 385-4168; Patti and Bill Wickline, owners. Seven rooms tastefully decorated, private and shared baths. Open all year. Rates: $42 to $79. Includes generous continental breakfast of fresh breads such as gingerbread, scones or coffeecake, and fruits. Children over twelve; no pets; Visa/MasterCard. Lizzie's brand of soaps and lotions available for purchase.

DIRECTIONS: from the Port Townsend Ferry take a right onto Water St., in one block take a left onto Taylor St. At the fountain, turn left onto Washington St. Proceed up the hill and turn right onto Pierce and proceed six blocks. From the south, at the third Port Townsend stoplight take a left onto Taylor St. and proceed as above.

Tasteful Victorian furnishings make Charlie's Room a favorite.

BED & BREAKFAST ASSOCIATIONS

Many innkeepers have formed associations to cooperatively promote their inns. Two such organizations are **Bed and Breakfast Innkeepers of Northern California (BBINC)** and **Bed and Breakfast Innkeepers of Southern California (BBISC)**. They have developed specific criteria for bed and breakfast inns. For a list of participating inns, contact:

BED & BREAKFAST INNKEEPERS OF NORTHERN CALIFORNIA: 2030 Union Street, Suite 310, San Francisco, CA 94123; (415) 563-4667.

BED & BREAKFAST INNKEEPERS OF SOUTHERN CALIFORNIA, P.O. Box 15385, Los Angeles, CA 90015-0385; (805) 966-0589.

On a regional level, neighboring innkeepers have organized to promote their inns and the area they are in. For regional bed-and-breakfast inn information, contact:

BED & BREAKFAST INNS OF AMADOR COUNTY, 215 Court Street, Jackson, CA 95642; (209) 223-0416. (Free brochure available)

BED & BREAKFAST INNS OF THE GOLD COUNTRY, P.O. Box 1375, Murphys, CA 95247; (209) 728-2897. (Brochure available for SASE, legal size envelope)

INNS OF THE GOLD COUNTRY, P.O. Box 322, Ione, CA 95640.

BED & BREAKFAST INNS OF HUMBOLDT COUNTY, P.O. Box CA-40, Ferndale, CA 95536; (707) 786-4000. (Free brochure available; packet of area information available for $1)

MONTEREY PENINSULA BED & BREAKFAST ASSOCIATION, 598 Laine Street, Monterey, CA 93940; (408) 375-8284. (Free packet of brochures available)

THE INNS OF POINT REYES, P.O. Box 145, Inverness, CA 94937; (415) 663-1420. (Free brochure available)

ASSOCIATION OF BED & BREAKFAST INNKEEPERS OF SAN FRANCISCO, 737 Buena Vista West, San Francisco, CA 94117; (415) 861-3008. (Brochure available for SASE, legal size envelope)

BED & BREAKFAST INNKEEPERS GUILD OF SANTA BARBARA, P.O. Box 20246, Santa Barbara, CA 93120. (Free brochure available)

BED & BREAKFAST INNKEEPERS OF SANTA CRUZ, P.O. Box 464, Santa Cruz, CA 95061-0464; (408) 425-1818. (Free brochure available)

WINE COUNTRY INNS OF SONOMA COUNTY, P.O. Box 51, Geyserville, CA 95441; (707) 433-INNS. (Free brochure available)

BED & BREAKFAST INNS OF THE UPPER NAPA VALLEY, P.O. Box 2147, Yountville, CA 94599.

HISTORIC COUNTRY INNS OF THE MOTHER LODE, P.O. Box 106, Placerville, CA 95667; (916) 626-5840.

BED & BREAKFAST INNS OF THE MARIN COAST, P.O. Box 145, Inverness, CA 94937.

MENDOCINO COAST INNKEEPERS ASSOCIATION, P.O. Box 128, Westport, CA 95488; (707) 964-2931. (Brochure available for $1 postpaid)

BED & BREAKFAST ASSOCIATION OF NAPA VALLEY, 1834 First Street, Napa, CA 94559; (707) 257-1051. (Brochure available for $1.50 postpaid)

SACRAMENTO INNKEEPERS ASSOCIATION, 2209 Capitol Avenue, Sacramento, CA 95816; (916) 441-3214. (Free brochure available)

UNIQUE NORTHWEST COUNTRY INNS, P.O. Box 2326, Salem, OR 97308

BED & BREAKFAST RESERVATION AGENCIES

The concept of Bed and Breakfast in the United States is rapidly expanding. To facilitate this phenomenon, reservation agencies are quickly cropping up, resulting in rapidly changing information. Many of the agencies listed below have been in existence for some time; others have been organized recently. Do not be surprised if there are changes when you contact them.

California

AMERICAN FAMILY INN/BED AND BREAKFAST SAN FRANCISCO, P.O. Box 349, San Francisco, CA 94101; (415) 931-3083; Richard and Susan Kreibich. Call Monday to Friday 9 A.M. to 5 P.M. Private residences and luxurious yachts. *San Francisco, Marin County, Carmel/ Monterey, the Wine Country, and Lake Tahoe.*

AMERICAN HISTORIC HOMES BED & BREAKFAST, P.O. Box 336, Dana Point, CA 92629; (714) 496-7050; Deborah Sakach. 9 A.M. to 5 P.M. National landmarks, plantations, seaside cottages, and Queen Anne cottages. *California, including Los Angeles and San Francisco; New York City, Boston, and Washington, D.C.*

THE BEAZLEY HOUSE, 1910 First Street, Napa, CA 94559; (707) 257-1051; Jim and Carol Beazley. Victorian homes and farm houses. *Napa Valley.*

BED AND BREAKFAST EXCHANGE, P.O. Box 88, St. Helena, CA 94574; (707) 963-7756; Diane Byrne, manager. *Cottages and small inns in the Napa and Sonoma wine country.*

BED AND BREAKFAST HOMESTAY, P.O. Box 326, Cambria, CA 93428; 805-927-4613; Alex Laputz. Call any time. Ocean views and secluded custom-built homes. *Hearst Castle area and California central coastal region.*

BED AND BREAKFAST INTERNATIONAL, 151 Ardmore Road, Kensington, CA 94707; (415) 525-4569; Jean Brown. 8:30 A.M. to 5 P.M. PST weekdays; 9 A.M. to noon on Saturdays. Private homes, apartments, houseboats, penthouses. *California, Hawaii, Seattle, Las Vegas, Chicago, New York City, and Washington, D.C.*

BED AND BREAKFAST OF LOS ANGELES, 32127 Harborview Lane, Westlake Village, CA 91361; (818) 889-7325— Peg Marshall. (818) 889-8870—Angie Kobabe. *Los Angeles area coastline from San Diego to San Francisco.*

CALIFORNIA HOUSEGUESTS INTERNATIONAL, INC., 18533 Burbank Blvd., P.O. Box 190, Tarzana, CA 91356; (818) 344-7878; Trudi Alexy. Apartments and mansions with ocean and mountain views. *San Diego, greater Los Angeles, Santa Monica, Malibu, Santa Barbara, Carmel/Monterey, San Francisco, Wine Country.*

CAROLYN'S BED & BREAKFAST HOMES, P.O. Box 84776, San Diego, CA 92138; (619) 435-5009; Carolyn Moellar. 9 A.M. to 6 P.M. *San Diego.*

CHRISTIAN BED AND BREAKFAST OF AMERICA, P.O. Box 388, San Juan Capistrano, CA 92693; (714) 496-7050; Call from 9 A.M. to 5 P.M. *Homes in 200 cities, including Los Angeles, Anchorage, Washington, D.C.*

CO-HOST, AMERICA'S BED & BREAKFAST, 11715 S. Circle Drive, Whittier, CA 90601; (213) 699-8427; Coleen Davis. 8 A.M. to 9 P.M. Mountain, beach, and in-town residences. *Covers the whole of California.*

EYE OPENERS BED & BREAKFAST RESERVATIONS, Box 694, Altadena, CA 91001; (213) 684-4428 or (818) 797-2055. Ruth Judkins and Elizabeth Cox. 9 A.M. to 6 P.M. *Private homes and bed and breakfast inns throughout California.*

VALLEY ACCOMMODATIONS, P.O. Box 3061, Yountville, CA 94599; (707) 944-0091; Jean Keenan. *Napa/Sonoma area*

Oregon

BED AND BREAKFAST ACCOMMODATIONS—OREGON PLUS, 5733 S.W. Dickinson Street, Portland, OR 97219; (503) 245-0642; Marcelle Tebo. *Locations throughout Oregon and southern Washington.*

NORTHWEST BED AND BREAKFAST TRAVEL UNLIMITED (established 1979), 610 S.W. Broadway, Suite 609, Portland, OR 97205; (503) 243-7616; Laine Friedman and Gloria Shaich. 9 A.M. to 5 P.M. weekdays. Farms, ranches, Victorian, contemporary, mountain, and ocean front homes. International listings. *Coverage extends throughout the United States and Canada.* Includes Bed and Breakfast tours of Great Britain.

Washington

PACIFIC BED & BREAKFAST, 701 N.W. 60th Street, Seattle, WA 98107; (206) 784-0539; Irmgard Castleberry. 9 A.M. to 5 P.M. weekdays. Mansions, Victorians, island cottages, and contemporary lakefront homes. *Covers Pacific Northwest.*

TRAVELLERS' BED & BREAKFAST, P.O. Box 492, Mercer Island, WA 98040; (206) 232-2345; Jean Knight. 8:30 A.M. to 5 P.M. daily. Guest houses, inns, and private residences. *Over 130 accommodations in the Pacific Northwest, including Vancouver and Victoria, British Columbia.*